SHATTERPROOF

The Countless Lives of Sheriff Rick

PREMISE

This is an original non-fiction narrative of Richard Grimstead, a contemporary Pacific Northwest Hero. No group of Hollywood writers could invent a more compelling make-believe character.

His daring exploits would make the late crazy motorcycle stuntman Evel Knievel sit up in his grave and tip his crash helmet towards him.

I decided to tell our hero's life story as a suspense narrative. Grimstead's life is the poster child for a Hollywood style suspense/thriller movie.

The marquee over the box office might read...
"Shatterproof... the Countless Lives of Sheriff Rick."

At first, it was to be *'the Nine Lives of Sheriff Rick,'* but both titles would be grossly undersold.

Skagit County Washington's two term Sheriff Richard Grimstead is a real example of an extraordinary person.

Who hasn't said...? "I know a Weird-Willey or a Naughty-Nancy. Their adventures, or escapades, would make a great book or movie."

The lifeblood of all T.V. reality shows is placing ordinary people, like you and me, into unbelievable situations.

And not unlike the reality show Survivor, the story and happenings in Rick Grimstead's life is for real.

Here are a few highlights of his many escapades:

At just thirteen, he spent a month chasing down, corralling and breaking *Rego*, an ornery wild range gelding. Then to make him run, he accidentally set fire to thousands of wilderness acres in Washington State.

While attending Washington State University, Rick's numerous sophomoric pranks got him expelled.

While living a type of *ski bum* or *Life of Riley* existence, he survived several late night car crashes, sending a couple buddies to the hospital. Rick also survived extreme high dives to impress a crowd of onlookers.

After his famous father, at least famous at WSU, pulled some strings and got Rick readmitted back into WSU. He took on some risky summer jobs, including working on a rock crusher, and dismantling missile silos. Ignoring many safety orders, Rick barely survived high falls and later being crushed to death. And there would have been no trace of him to claim... except maybe a few telltale blood stains.

As a broke, bone-tired, overworked, newly married young man, he crashed his car into the bottom of a thirty-foot deep irrigation canal.

In Vietnam, he was awarded twenty-nine Air Medals, while flying six hundred helicopter combat missions.

After completing his tour in Nam, he saved his flight crew and scores of Hawaiian sunbathers from sudden death, redirecting a harrowing helicopter crash.

While on duty as a Washington State Trooper, he had several narrow escapes from out-of-control drivers. When Sheriff Rick retired after two elected terms,

I approached him about telling his life story.

At first, he declined saying ... "au shucks my life's no big deal." His family and everyone else that have heard his exploits, vibrantly disagreed.

When I asked his wife, Kay, about Rick's daredevil stunts, she said, "Rick doesn't have a death wish... he just thinks he can do anything."

*　*　*

PART ONE

OUT OF COUNTRY AT LAST

1

"OH MY GOD!" I yelled, locking my stare through the helicopter's thin Plexiglas canopy.

Just a hundred feet ahead... three high-tension steel reinforced cables... charged with fifty thousand volts of electricity... raced towards us at one hundred and forty miles per hour.

My battle reflex awakened, as I pulled back on the Cyclic control stick. The impulsive move I had used many times in Vietnam, to avoid the enemy and lift us out of harm's way.

The six tons of flying machinery lifted just high enough to steer clear and free of sudden death. Almost!

My expression was frozen. Not by fear, but by disbelief.

Why now? What will they say to Kay?

The finest flying machine in the United States Marine Corps had been neutered. Its forward motion slowed to a sickening metal grinding crawl... when...

The sounds of Snap... Bang... pulsed through the helicopter's cockpit. The sulfur smell of burnt metal and dazzling flashes of electrical arcs likened the experience to a Steppenwolf rock concert. It had also been a mind-blowing foreshadowing of things to come. However, this was not like their song '*Magic Carpet Ride...*' much closer to '*Rock Me!*'

If I could have chosen a Steppenwolf song to fit the moment it would have been... 'It's Never Too Late!'

But this time it was...

Much too little!

Much too late!

* * *

Power lines... hundreds of feet above the canyon below.

EARLIER THAT MORNING:

I was Rick Grimstead, and had fulfilled my yearlong combat tour in Vietnam. I had put in for my three new duty choices. Pensacola, Florida was my first choice, and Hawaii was my second choice, which I drew.

In 1970, I was only twenty-seven years old, but eons wiser in the ways of the world than the people back home, Many who were untouched by the horrors of brutal combat.

Above is a photo of me three years later... 1973.

What's ironic is my birthday had been as memorable as my near-death experience that day. Born Easter Sunday, April 25, 1943 was very special from the start. There is a less than a one percent chance Easter will fall on April 25th any given year. It can fall on any Sunday between March 22 and April 25. This is because Easter is celebrated on the first Sunday after the first full moon in the Northern Hemisphere.

Also ironic... the word Easter originated from the Hebrew word "Pesach" which means <u>Passover.</u>

This is what I had tried to actually do.

<u>*Pass our sorry butts over*</u> the deadly power lines racing towards us.

Easter lore reads... Children born on Easter Day are said to be lucky. Also it is said that a wind that blows on Easter Day, will continue to blow throughout the year.

Like maybe a baby boy blow hard may have been born on that day... just saying.

*   *   *

December 7, 1970 found me co-piloting a Boeing CH 46 Sea Knight twin rotor helicopter on my *'Fam-flight.'* It had been twenty-nine years to the day, since the Japanese bombed Pearl Harbor.

Having served my required time, in the beyond crazy war zone... being shot at, in almost all of my six-hundred missions... timer-set bombs planted under my bed... etc.

I was now ready for some carefree flights in friendly skies. With blue skies, fluffy white clouds, maybe having to dodge around a small flock of pretty lovebirds, coming home to feed their young?

The *Fam-flight* was the routine process of familiarizing of pilots, cycling out of their Vietnam tours of duty, with the local landmarks and sights. This training flight was required of all the Vietnam, mission completed, helicopter pilots who would serve as aircraft flight commanders out of the Kaneohe Bay Marine Base in Oahu, Hawaii.

Aircraft flight commander, O'Brien, piloted the massive machine. I sat next to him in the copilot seat. Crew chief Jenkins, our only passenger, stood behind us holding onto the handle of the slightly ajar entrance door.

Jenkins gazed out at the tropical countryside below, whisking by at one hundred and twenty-five knots.

O'Brien pointed out various landmarks as we cruised along Oahu's north shore. "There is this and there is that," summed up his descriptions along the scenic coastline as we neared its completion for this journey for this fresh new guy, who was new to the island's easy living.

We had been airborne only thirty minutes, with his narrator's bullshit in high gear, when it came to describing his own flying ability. I had basic Marine Corp first-aid training, but had diagnosed O'Brien with a terminal case of diarrhea of the mouth.

I had told O'Brien about my interest in the surfing culture, having learned that skill when in flight school in Pensacola, Florida. Later I spent every free moment I had between combat flights, on the Marine base's remote semi-secure Vietnam beach.

"Waimea Beach... the Pipe Line," O'Brien said turning the copter inland across the sandy beach below. "The Polynesian Culture Center," he motioned with a head bob.

"Cool!" I said, straining my neck to look back at the breakers pounding Waimea Beach.

The big twin rotor helicopter crossed the Kamehameha Highway following the flow of the Waimea River inland.

We flew north and well above the two hundred foot high canyon rims that defined Waimea Valley.

"Waihi Falls," O'Brien spouted, nodding a glance at me. "In Hawaiian it means 'trickling falls.'

"Not exactly Niagara," I grinned back, checking out the water plunging about fifty feet into a large emerald colored pool with a dozen people swimming and enjoying the idyllic Hawaiian December afternoon, "But still real cool."

O'Brien made the chopper perform a wide sweeping turn, heading us back down the river valley towards Waimea Beach.

Jenkins and I busied ourselves, checking out the beauty spread out below, as we soared towards Waimea Beach.

"Check out the bare breasted wahines swimming in the water," Jenkins blurted out.

And I did, like any red- blooded battle weary marine would have. My thoughts then returned to my gorgeous wife waiting for my return this afternoon, and the surf on Oahu's North Shore, known for its massive waves. I was always ready or challenging, and high-risk adventures in life. The North Shore was dangerous for inexperienced surfers, because of massive coral formations near the surface. The North Shore during the winter months could present the risk of serious injury, but was on my acceptable cost/reward meter. *Better some great fun than 'sorry I didn't,'* or something like that.

I thought it would be better to start out as a *Haole,* Hawaiian for outsider. Soon, after the locals witnessed my surfing skills, I would become the Big Wave *Kahuna,* Hawaiian for the high priest, or wizard.

Like every new thing I attempted in life, I imagined myself as the next *wizard of surfing.*

The aircraft commander put on his tour guide persona and for an instant forgetting, he was piloting a Boeing Vertol CH-46D. The twin T-58-GE-10 turbo shaft engines rated at 1,400 shp and could carry 25 troops or 7,000 pounds of cargo.

The copter's previous versions were called the *Flying Banana*, but this six-million- dollar instrument of war was more of an airborne hot chili pepper on steroids. It was not made for pleasure, sightseeing, or tourist-island hopping, even if used on an official search, and' lookie-see' mission for this new guy.

O'Brien continued to point out the sights below... taking his eyes away from the fast approaching danger. My exclamation about God made him freeze at the controls.

The loud snapping of steel cables and the sensation of falling, snapped O'Brien back from shock to the reality of regaining control of his helicopter.

"I got it!" O'Brien yelled at me, his stern faced copilot who had moved the cyclic back up, to try and miss the power lines.

Outside of the chopper, the severed, high-tension lines fell to the earth, across the North Coast's special tourist jewel... Waimea Beach. The whipping swords of steel cut through vegetation, and a Life Guard stand, while snapping blinding flashes at anything coming in contact with its fifty-thousand volts of sudden death.

"Yeah well... all the gages are fried." I said, but still not sure, if I should surrender the controls. As the helicopter leveled off, I reluctantly gave back total control to flight commander O'Brien.

"Crew Chief!" O'Brien barked.

"Grimstead is right... I got nothing!"

The deep blue Pacific spread out below us to the horizon and the horrors of the jungles of Vietnam, safely over six-thousand miles away.

Those awful black clouds from air strikes, and burning napalm *'in country'*, were replaced by the white fluffy cumulus clouds accentuated in a travel agent's version of a paradise found. The only stain on perfection... a trailing black tail of smoldering oil from the Sea Knight's engine compartment.

We counted our lucky stars, invisible in the gorgeous daytime sky... but burned bright in out spinning minds. O'Brien banked the wounded bird back towards Oahu and along the five miles leading to Kaneohe Bay Marine Base. Each of us praying, to whatever God, or thought, that would deliver him home safe. All wondering how many lives may have been lost at Waimea Beach.

It was a weekday... maybe not as many as a weekend? However, even if we did survive the journey back to base...
we were all still in deep shit.

2

"THAT DEATH DEFYING HELICOPTER F... ING HIGH WIRE STUNT...

may cost you assholes your commissions," Squadron Commander Reynolds said, shaking his head and lighting another cigarette.

"Six combat trained Marine eyes couldn't see three damn dirty power cables humming in the clear blue f...ing sky?" He took a deep drag then crushed out the cigarette and continued. "Better lucky than smart I guess? Nobody died... except for a couple of dogs belonging to a Hippie guy. And those were the main power lines for the entire north side of Oahu. Normal electrical power will for be out for weeks... we had to send in our construction engineers to help with temporary power."

We both exhaled and sucked in deep breaths as Reynolds continued...

"I should deduct the six million bucks you cost the Corp and who knows how much for the power lines... from your stinking pay."

O'Brien and I stood silent next to the parked helicopter while Commander Reynolds walked away to his waiting jeep. As he was driven away by his driver, we could still see the disgust on his face.

The sad sack chopper, which was now the not so stellar looking Sea Knight, sat in the hanger. A swarm of mechanics checked out the damage from my ill-fated *Fam-flight.*

Crew Chief Jenkins approached us holding a clip board and said. "Lucky... lucky. Take a look at the fuel cells."

I walked over and ran my hand over the helicopter's aluminum skin, where the rivets held the fuel cells in place. "The rivet heads are all burnt off. What kept the fuel from spilling out and exploding?" I asked.

"A higher power? Just dumb luck?" Jenkins said, shaking his head in disbelief.

"Is it a total Chief?" I asked.

"We'll use it for parts. All the electronics are burnt to a crisp. The skin is warped real bad... Canopy looks like a slave's back, flogged with a steel whip. Maybe Jesus looked worst.

We rolled ours eyes at his lame remark. Jenkins continued, "She had lots of hours. But the reason the C.O. is so pissed... I guess, is the bad press will be another... bigger... much bigger, a real nightmare for the base."

"We'll all be lucky to survive this," O'Brien said. I glared at the asshole running his mouth that got us into this mess.

O'Brien was an amateur troublemaker.

But I had my Black-Belt in stirring-the-pot.

The Olympic Champion of making mischief.

Any trouble brought on me, had to be of my own choosing. Bullshit trouble caused by others I didn't need.

"I'm gonna go get a drink... anyone else?" O'Brien pointed to the exit.

I looked at Jenkins who said, "I'm only a Crew Chief... but maybe hanging with you two... not smart right now."

"Sometimes being a flight Commander... doesn't make you a smart guy." I said.

O'Brien walked away, getting our message...

Earth to big shot... drop dead!

* * *

3

SURF'S UP

TWO WEEKS LATER: The Congo Green 1965 Volkswagen Kombi followed the twisting canyon road that led down to tie into the highway, fronting Waimea Beach.

I gazed out at the beauty of this tropical paradise.

My arm rested on the rolled down passenger windowsill. The sparkling clean VW Bus, I sat in, was captained by my wife Kay. She steered our ride, serpentine style like a real pro, towards the beach.

I thought of myself as Tarzan, and Kay as my Jane and best friend.

But unlike Tarzan... the monkey slash chimpanzee named *'Cheeta'* was also played by goofball me.

Kay had befriended Sharon, one of the other base wives, who offered their car for the day. Sharon's hubby was both a pilot and a surfer complete with a surfboard, but he had to work that day. Nevertheless, being a nice person of sorts, I rescued his surfboard from the dark confines of their garage and brought it along to play with me at the beach.

Kay knew better than most about my need for speed. Not just for flying, but in everything I tried. And she was not about to let me drive Sharon's car.

To chauffer her wanta-be surfer to his day catching the big waves... suited her just fine.

*   *   *

The result of our messed up 'Fam-Flight' was life changing for us three stooges.

And even though I thought of myself as a victim of O'Brien's screw up, the Marine Corp found us all culpable in the black eye stain we created with the local folks.

I received a letter of caution added to my file, for my part in the mishap and was still able to fly for the rest of my time in Hawaii.

Unlike me, O'Brien didn't fare as well, and was grounded for a year with a black mark in his career file. Jenkins got a negative letter added to his file s well. Not a plus for the two career Marines. I was mustering out of the Marine Corps in two months and cared less.

Jenkins's statement about them being 'Lucky... lucky,' was an understatement.

If the power lines had hit the rotary blades, the cables would have been ripped apart, wrapping around the twisting exploding helicopter. The ensuing fire ball would drop to Waimea Beach, killing many sunbathers.

If the power lines had hit below the rotary blade and struck the canopy, the steel cables would have cut through the cockpit resulting in the same deadly falling fireball.

However, by luck or Devine intervention, when I pulled back on the controls lifting the bird a little, the power lines slammed into the only place on the helicopter that it could survive.

In over a one in a million shot, the high voltage cables struck the eighteen-inch high metal frame member between the rotary blades and the plastic chin bubble.

Between the pulling of the Sea Knight and the fifty-thousand volt cables arcing, as they touched, allowed the cables to burn apart upon impact. Freeing the wounded, but flyable, helicopter to recover and limp away.

The scrambling Waimea Beach sunbathers were saved from sudden death by Physics.

The fifty-thousand volt cables were smaller in diameter than other high voltage power lines of the day. Any larger and they would have brought down the helicopter, killing hundreds.

When the cables parted two-hundred feet up in the air, they fell, widening the gap on the beach where most of the sunbathers lay. Miraculously the cables missed the sunbathers.

The point where the helicopter hit the cables was much closer to one side of the canyon.

The shorter side was the side still energized, hitting the ground short of the highway and ripping into mostly empty parked cars.

The people in some of the cars hit, by the cables, were spared because of the vehicle's rubber tires.

The longer cables, on the other side, became de-energized steel swords falling towards the ground ripping mostly vegetation and splashing onto the river.

A lifeguard was the only injured person. One of the de-energized cables slapped into the side of his lifeguard stand.

The stunned young man face planted into the sand breaking his life ring-tossing arm.

The only losses of life were two mongrel dogs belonging to a Hippie couple. The Hippies tied their dogs to the rear bumper of an old VW Bus. One of the falling energized cables glanced off the Bus, struck a spare jerry gas can on the bumper and burst the psychedelic colored party wagon into flames.

* * *

"Hey stop... stop," I said opening my door before Kay came to a stop.

"Smooth Jocko... could have waited..."

"... No look!" I pointed to a couple horses with riders on a bluff overlooking the highway and trotting towards the beach.

I got out while Kay parked the VW Bus. She caught up to where I stood next to a large palm tree on the road shoulder.

"Looks just like him... don't it?" Kay asked, in almost a trance I watched the two youngsters run their horses through the sandy ground covered coast.

"Same blaze... same white stockings on the hind legs. Not as fast... not even close," I said turning away and returning to the Kombi.

Kay gave me some space, then returned and drove us towards Waimea Beach.

It had been five years since I had to part with the only thing I had ever cared for, near as much as Kay. Tough thing being a grown-up... doing grown-up things.

Ten minutes later Kay parked the Bus along the highway, near Waimea Beach.

I shouldered the borrowed ten-foot surfboard. Kay carried the picnic basket she had prepared for our special day.

We passed by the roped off remains of the Hippie's Vee-Dub psychedelic painted van.

"Those poor doggies," Kay said.

"How about all the good Maui Wowie gone to waste?" I asked, kicking through the burnt debris inside the roped off damage area.

"Careful Rick... ya might get a contact high and fall off your surfboard later," Kay laughed, spurring away swinging her picnic basket.

"Ya know I'd never be the one to take a chance like that."

"And your tour in Vietnam was like a peaceful stroll in Nirvana or dancing with the caged lightning in those steel cables... a day in the park?"

I grabbed my surfboard and sprinted towards the water yelling to her, "Surfs up Iolani... got a go!"

*   *   *

4

BONZI BUNGEE CORD

The next hour found me abused by the monster winter waves. I straddled the board, my feet in the water waiting for another set of waves to come in. The saltwater stinging, everyplace the coarse shard scraped flesh from me. Over two dozen body slams and counting.

I wiped my brow and shook my head to clear my vision. Reaching down I felt my right ankle rubbed raw by the surfboard's surgical tubing.

I need to add a piece of something soft as a foothold... to my invention, I thought.

I had two seven day R&Rs (rest and reload as some guys called it) from Nam to Hawaii during my tour *'in country,'* Vietnam.

While surfing on my first R&R, all I seemed to do was chase my board every time after I was knocked off. Then, just by luck, I was walking by our neighbor's garage and saw him supporting some sporting equipment to his car's roof rack with some rubber tubing. I was fascinated by the items bouncing back into place as he shifted them around. A light went on in my head.

And the next day he brought me home a twelve-foot length of surgical tubing from his work. He was a doctor and had been using it for years.

Unbeknownst to me, I had just invented the surfboard bungee cord retriever.

The Hawaiians that saw me use it were blown away, because they had never seen one before.

So as I stroked my sore ankle... I smiled to myself having given back something to the surfing Gods. Like they say, *funny how desperate times can create some cool things.*

Me catching a wave, I was having fun again.

On the shore stood a teenage boy and girl mounted on their horses. The girl sat on a painted pony. The boy sat on a horse that had my attention. *A fifteen hand tall sorrel with a blaze on my face and staring at him.*

The sorrel snorted and shook his mane. "Couldn't be," I laughed.

As if they heard me, the two riders turned and galloped their steeds up the beach and out of sight. I sighed and rolled my head around to relieve the tension of too much surfing.

The constant ocean swell caused the long surfboard to rise and fall, like a smooth ride on a fast running stallion. I pressed my inner thighs tight against the surfboard to remain upright.

A loud roar of an approaching jet airplane from the Marine Base, made me turn and watch the fighter lift up and head out to sea. The jet's fiery afterburning caught my attention. It reminded me of a long ago event. I laughed again, "I give up... too funny."

Time was a friend I had now... and I took some to reflect on my life. I was only twenty-seven years old at the time... but had lots of stuff to mull over.

* * *

PART TWO

BOYHOOD DREAMS

5

FOURTEEN YEARS EARLIER:

WOOSH! THE BLAZING BALL OF FIRE consumed every obstacle in its path, while matching all the twists and turns of the ground-strafing missile.

Nonstop tall clusters of bone-dry underbrush were smashed to kindling by the beast before ignited by its trailing torch.

The young man, straddling the open range rocket, dug both his knees into its forward flank. He pulled back hard on the control reigns, trying to steer the beast hell-bent to escape the pursuing inferno.

Realizing the futility of not being in command, he released the brute and gave into his ride's need for more speed.

A gleam came into the young man's eyes. His mission accomplished, the two were now one. The young man remembered an old naval war saying for times like these...

'Damn the torpedoes...full speed ahead!'

His euphoria...was short lived. The fireball, just fifteen feet behind him, had worked its way up the tentacle pulling across his leg. Suddenly the fireball planted its scorching fury deep into the fork of a small tree.

The comet's burning appendage jerked tight, yanking the young man sideways. With his free hand, he ripped the tether free.

The two conquistadors, emancipated from the fireball, were fueled by adrenalin. They resumed the race to nowhere, disappearing from the firestorm in a cloud of prairie dust. The hot choking smoke around their escape path, was replaced with cool refreshing air dancing across the fast approaching irrigation canal

Proud of his accomplishment, this young man glanced back at the countryside laid waste by his foolhardy journey, coming back to my reality.

This might not play well with the powers to be.

* * *

6

THE "C" STREET SIGN SNAPPED OFF... spinning from its wooden post.

Ephrata Washington's fire engine number-two was racing toward the growing inferno. Cutting the corner too sharp, it bounced over the curb, splintering the signpost like a large buffalo plowing through cane reeds on his way to cool off in the Congo River.

The metal sign banged on the asphalt, the letter "C" a possible symbol for the "Calamity" that may lie ahead.

The fire truck's siren blaring, passed by a dozen single story ramblers lining both sides of the dead end street, before entering the dusty dirt road leading into the low hill country.

The overpowering odor of hot cremated vegetation... everywhere.

The day before, a stiff breeze had funneled out of the higher hills to the south. Today, sending the first whiff of burnt bunchgrass and sagebrush to the residents of Ephrata, Almost as if it was just a dream... not real, but real it was.

The wildfire raced through the dry standing brushwood, just four hundred yards from the city's southern boundary, snapping its fiery tongue like a snake searching out its prey.

* * *

7

MY ACCOMPLICE

Art Hunt looked like a budding adolescent lad that had never missed a meal. However, on this hot August afternoon, his little on the chunky twelve-year old thoughts was not dreaming about what's for dinner.

Art, wearing dirty jeans and a dirty white tee shirt, stood under the only shade at the end of 'C' street, a weathered old red oak tree.

Two jackrabbits bolted from the brush land, zigzagging away from Art and disappeared back into brush away from the smoke funneling into 'C' street.

"Crap!" Art said, letting out a breath held in too long while digging out crusty dust balls from his nostrils with a trigger finger.

"Sure did the trick," an unseen person's voice said, startling the already nervous as hell juvenile.

I ambled up next to him, the sparkling whites of my eyes stood out like the sparkling whites of my eyes, in a face layered with wind blown chocolate dust and smoke, standing out like a photography film negative of piss holes in a snow bank.

"It was your idea," Art said, turning to see people walking towards them.

"Don't say a word!"

"What if my dad asks?"

I turned away from Art. "Friends never rat on each other," I whispered back to Art, whose feet were frozen in place from guilt.

I winked at Art, then crossed to the far side of the street and headed home, just two houses away. I had often thought of myself as a young man out of control, yet somehow removed from my misdeeds.

I had a lot of sweat equity invested in my fifteen-hand tall wild sorrel horse, besides the fifty hard, earned dollars I paid to old man Fred Jones.

Not to mention the cuts, bruises, sprained ligaments, and a busted hump in catching, corralling and breaking the ornery critter.

After all the long hours of perfecting my dream horse, there was just one flaw. Not a flaw, like a small blemish on an otherwise stunning diamond, or a Knick in the lacquered-mirror like finish of a brand new Porsche.

Rego's flaw, to me, was more like the Grand Canyon's mile-deep ten-mile wide scar cut into the otherwise pristine rolling green hills of Northern Arizona.

Rego just... would NOT run!

I taught Rego to walk with the weight of a rider, to follow the slightest tug on the reins to any direction, to trot, to gallop, and even backup, but, oh no! Never run, even when I dug in my spurs or swatted his flank with the reins.

What's a speed junky gonna do?

In John Steinbeck's 1937 Novel *'Of Mice and Men,'* Steinbeck borrowed a line from **Robert Burns**' poem *'To a Mouse,'* which read: *(The best laid schemes of mice and men/ Often go awry,)* or in my verson...

'Horseshit Happens.'

I had my own version of another old saying, *'You can lead a horse to water, but you can't make him drink... but if the horse thinks you set his tail on fire, you can make him run like hell!.'*

I knew that all wild animals were deathly afraid of fire, so I tied a rope around a large tumbleweed, mounted Rego, and had Art light the tumbleweed on fire, with a match.

The tumbleweed sat about twenty feet behind Rego, but the prevailing breeze was blowing the smoke away from the horse. Nothing happened. I tried pulling the burning bush closer to Rego. The horse didn't respond, still unaware of the danger behind him.

"Turn him towards the fire," yelled Art!

I nodded to Art, wrapping the free end of the rope around the saddle horn, and pulling Rego's head around enough for him see the blazing ball of fire, just ten feet behind.

Viola! The Roman candle, aka Rego, took off. Like the crowd of shoppers on black Friday at midnight, blowing past the barely open doors at Wal-Mart, with me hanging on for the ride of my life!

* * *

8

LOUISE L'AMOUR

Later, when I got home and walked into the kitchen, my mom was listening on the radio to... *'The Story of My Life,'* by Marty Robbins.

"Richard... better go check on your horse." Ada said, as luck would have it, pulling her attention away from Louis L'amour's novel, 'The Burning Hills.'

He tried to escape into the burning heat of the Texas Flat. There, in an isolated homestead, he found safety... and Maria Cristina, the extraordinary woman nursed him back to health.

Ada envisioned herself of wanting to be like Maria, but with a little more class.

* * *

Rego pranced around in his tiny enclosure.

The young horse was unsure of all the smoke in the air, and commotion. I stuck a hand through the boards to soothe my ridding partner. Rego would have none of it, pulling back and snorting.

We stared into each other's eyes, looking for any guilt.
"Not your fault Rego," I said, turning towards the house.

Ada stood in the doorway looking at me, wondering. She never asked me anything, didn't really want to know. Ada did not want to be the disciplinarian of the family.

She delegated this task to my father.

Mom and Dad in College.

Mom was the daughter of a prominent, wealthy, brokerage firm partner, in Seattle.

Her parent's home, on Lake Washington, came complete with two maids, a butler and a cook. Ada traded in her life of luxury, and became *the good wife*,' to her prince charming, football star husband.

Dad's job moved them, along with their four kids, to this remote Eastern Washington town of three thousand simple souls, and life styles.

Robert Sonju Grimstead, or just Bob to his friends and family was... a Washington State Trooper... a keeper of the peace. Dad was a *John Wayne, The Duke*,' type of man, in both stature and personality. Ada also wasn't going to be a spy on her kids either.

Big Bob could figure it out for himself.

*   *   *

9

SPORT OF KINGS

A volunteer firefighter, on his way back to the fire station, after shopping for the crews evening meal, noticed the puff of black smoke, in the afternoon sky.

Luckily for all, another half hour and the fire might have gotten out of control, burning away tens of thousands brushy acres.

As it turned out, over two thousand acres were scorched to the earth. The fire's origin became a mystery to the locals. Maybe an act of God, or something? Like an unheard lightning strike? Spontaneous combustion?

Ironic: In 1958, the number one songs on the Billboard charts were; *'Great Balls of Fire'* by Jerry Lee Lewis, in January, *'Secretly'* by Jimmy Rogers, in June, and *'Problems,'* by the Everly Brothers, in December.

In one misguided moment, I had accomplished all three.

When asked why I named my horse 'Rego?' I said, "I don't remember for sure. I think it was Spanish for something." Well the word 'Rey' is Spanish, meaning 'King,' and the GO part of 'Rego' might be from English, for in *'Go like hell!'*

After all, *'The Sport of Kings,'* is in fact *horseracing.*

Most people with great imaginations; dreamers, artists, architects, philosophers, are waiting for inspiration, or waiting for the world to come to them. Rocks and trees wait for the rain, sun, and wind to erode them, to shape them. Few people inspired by their surroundings, but not waiting for direction, are the doers in life.

The risk takers, the gamblers, the front-runners... they all are living for the moment.

Racecar drivers that imagine dangers ahead are the crashers... the losers.

The racers, zoned in on the task, trying to avoid the ordinary, seeking out the extra ordinary, become the winners.

No guts no glory...unless you spill your guts.

What reward or price is worth the risk?

My need for speed and carefree attitude brought me to this crossroad.

The risks taken today like in my young age, where mere child's play, compared to the death defying adventures awaiting Ephrata's boy wonder.

My buddy, Steve Englehorn and I sharing some laughs outside our 8th grade classroom, in Ephrata. Later, Steve became the bailiff for the Washington State Supreme Court.

By the way, there had only been seven or eight bailiffs for the Supreme Court, almost a lifetime appointment.

* * *

10

THE SEEDS OF YEARNING... planted deep into me, at an early age.

I came into this world as Richard Forbes Grimstead, in the winter of 1943. My middle name came from my maternal grandfather, James Forbes McBurney, a prominent Seattle stock brokerage firm partner in the 1920's.

In addition, maybe my grandfather's middle name had genetic makers attached to it, as well, for a risk taking life style. These markers were so powerful, because Ada, my mother, had been adopted. The traits must have gotten to me by osmosis, and not by a simple bloodline. Around 1915, James McBurney followed his dream of finding a homestead farm near Wendell, Idaho.

The lure of making a living in dirt soon waned. His outgoing personality earned him a shot at political office. He ran for the State Senate, almost winning, losing only by one vote. He made new friends, and was convinced to set his sights on the rising stock market trade, in Seattle.

McBurney, emboldened by a brush with fame, left his large Idaho land holdings in the hands of a young sharecropper.

The plan was simple; the sharecropper would pay the land taxes each year, in exchange for keeping the profits from the farm. This freed McBurney to seek his fortune in Seattle, and still hold onto the deed to thousands of acres of prime Idaho farmland.

McBurney talked his way into joining a rising Seattle brokerage firm, soon becoming a partner, riding the mad influx of investors to strike it rich, in the stock market.

He married Harriet Nichols, and bought a fine home in the upscale Mountlake Cut community, on Lake Washington in Seattle.

(The photos above... 1924)

James McBurney was a rich man, with a trophy wife, a chauffer, butler, and two maids. James and Harriet adopted a little baby girl, while farming in Idaho, completing their happy home. The little girl was my mother Ada.

The good life...for years was wonderful! Then...Boom! The 1929 Stock Market Crash.

Funny how a little thing, like the total collapse of the world economy, can ruin a person's life?

Goodbye to the fabulous income, from rising stock market sales.

Goodbye to the life of luxury; cars, yachts, and servants.

Finally, in 1935, his home on the water. He had paid almost fifty thousand dollars ten years before, and now had to sell for just twelve thousand dollars.

Even his ace in the hole, thousands of acres of Idaho farmland, was lost for unpaid property taxes.

The sharecropper did not pay the taxes for years, and never told McBurney, who was too busy doing fun things, to check up on his simple dirt investment.

Harriet was a schoolteacher, which helped fill the income gap, from her husband's miss-adventures.

McBurney got on a roller coaster of jobs, and failed investments. He worked as a pipe fitter, tried stock brokerage again, this time just an employee.

When he did get ahead once again, he lost it all when he bought into a salted gold mine, in Montana. For most of her childhood, Ada McBurney lived the life of a rich man's daughter. Her dad shielded her from the dark side, and she became use to being spoiled. Like any real princess, she was on the lookout for her prince charming.

*   *   *

Robert Sonju Grimstead, a six-foot-four, three-sport letterman in high school. He played football, and basketball, and ran track, where he won the state championship in high jump, shot put and 120-yard-high-hurdles.

Robert Grimstead was a real dream date, for all the young ladies that saw him, or just heard of him.

Bob, as everyone called him, received a full ride scholarship at Washington State University for football, later listed as one of the top 100 players ever to play WSU.

My Dad graduated in 1938, and played in the annual best of the college East West All Star's *Shrine Game* in San Francisco, California.

He contracted typhoid fever shortly after the game, almost dying, dropping from his playing weight of two hundred and sixty pounds, down to a mere one hundred and thirty pounds.

The New York Giants chose Bob Grimstead in the tenth round, of the 1938 NFL draft. He was the 88th player taken overall that year. Unfortunately, he did not recover in time from his ailment to play in the NFL.

His mom nursed him back to reasonable health, giving up his dream to play in the National Football League.

Bob joined the Washington State Patrol in 1939.

Dad Grimstead's parents were immigrants from Norway in the 1900's. His father's first job in the United States was an apprentice jeweler, in the small North Western Washington farming town of Edison. After learning his trade, he moved his family to Tacoma, Washington and opened his own jewelry store.

Dad and Mom were married and lived in Seattle. I was their first born and only son. Four daughters followed, Gail a year and half after me, and the next three were spaced about three years apart, Harriet, Christine and finally Nancy. From about five years old, I would watch people on horses trot by my house, on their way to the riding trails, on the outskirts of their Seattle neighborhood.

6 years old

When I was a little guy, I would approach a rider, who had stop to adjust something on his horse's riggings and ask, "Hey mister can I pet your horse?" If they granted him permission, my next question was always, "Can I sit on him... please?"

Very few equestrians could resist the cute little guy, wearing a shit eatin' grin, and sparkles in my eyes.

My mom would take us to see cowboy movie heroes like Gene Autry, Roy Rogers, Tom Mix, Hopalong Cassidy, The Lone Ranger and many more.

I was hooked! I begged my parents constantly for ridding lessons.

When I grew bigger, they relented, and I became a regular student at the *Rainwater Stables*, in Lake City, just north of Seattle.

The only problem, the horses were sluggish, meant for women and scared children.

But not a future member of '*Ghost Riders in the Sky.*'

I yearned to be a fun lovin' fast ridin' cowboy...

someday soon... real soon.

*   *   *

11

TO THE PROMMISED LAND of milk and honey... but was more like sagebrush and sunny!

In the spring of 1958, Dad told our family he was being transferred to Ephrata, in Eastern Washington.

Ephrata was the Grant County Seat, with a population of four thousand and five hundred folks. Ephrata was two hundred miles from Seattle and Ada's family.

Ephrata had won the county seat by getting the representative from a rival community drunk.

The rep made a fool of himself, when presenting his town's competing presentation to the state legislature.

The town's first official name was simply '*Station 11 Water Stop*,' where the Great Northern Railroad ran through, between two rocky hills. The water supply was drawn from the nearby natural water spring called '*Beezley Springs*.'

A worker for the railroad said the orchards and the landscape were similar to the Holy Land. He called the area "*Ephrata*"- Hebrew for "*fruitful*," which is another name for Bethlehem.

The Grand Coulee Dam, on the Columbia, transformed the community into a government town in 1933.

The U.S. Army Air Corps built a large training base there in 1942. After WW2, the Columbia Basin Project delivered water from Grand Coulee Dam to over 600,000 acres of fertile, dry, farmland.

At the same time, the Grant County utility district began construction of two great hydroelectric dams on the Columbia River. The two large hydroelectric dams provided Grant County with cheap, clean, reliable power.

The massive government projects brought growth, prosperity, talented people and their families to Ephrata.

The Robert Grimstead's would be the latest immigrants, but not all seeking the holy grail of adventure.

Ada Grimstead loved to read about the old west. Living the role of a dusty dressed prairie wife, with five snotty nosed kids, while her lawman husband was dealing with highway crime in modern times, was not exactly her *cup-of-tea.*

Ephrata's Native American name was '*Tukta-hyos-pum*,' interpreted by the first white settlers to mean '*Indian Graves.*

In Ada's thoughts, the burial place of the good life she had grown up with in the big city.

In my eyes, when there is Indians, there must be cowboys, and where there is cowboys... horses..."*Yippee!*"

* * *

12

ANGLING FOR A HORSE RIDE

I sat on the swimming pool's boarder lip, leaning back with my palms, on the hot concrete deck.

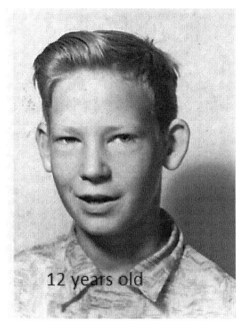

12 years old

A little bored, I began bouncing my heels underwater, off the tiled wall to the beat of the music playing in my mind.

Ernie Johnson swam up to me, grabbing a hold of the pool edge. A wave of cool pool water splashed this daydreaming, fourteen-year-old newcomer back to the present. "Sorry guy!" Ernie said, wiping water off his face with a free hand.

I gave him a disgusted look, before sensing the opportunity to ask what's cool around Ephrata.

"No big deal... you live around here?"

"Nah... but not real far," Ernie said, "I live on a farm, outside of town."

"Do you have any horses?"

Ernie looked at me in a strange way, for an instant, then said, "Yeah... we have two."

"Can I come out and ride them?"

Ernie smiled at my boldness, "Sure."

"When?"

Ernie climbed out of the pool, and sat back down next to me, not sure what to say, "Maybe..."

"How 'bout after swimming?" I asked, self-assured and not letting Ernie think, or put me off, or say no.

Don't blow it stupid... make him think you like him, I thought.

Ernie took a deep breath and laughed, "Sure... but you'll have to get there yourself. Our car will be full goin' home."

After Mrs. Johnson drove away, with her family in their car, I took a look at the map, she had given him.

'It's only eight miles... and Ernie has two horses... no problem,' I figured.

The hot summer breeze dried my skin as I pedaled my bike, like one of the hydroelectric turbine blades spinning below the Grand Coulee Dam, on the Columbia River.

With each passing mile, my anticipation of riding one of Ernie's horses revved my mental motor to the max. *Yippee,* I dreamed... what's next for me.

My dream became real. I spent my free time ridding every day that Ernie's parents would let him. Ernie didn't have any saddles. We rode bareback, and soon learned how to run like the wild Indian braves I had seen, in the old west movies.

Ernie and I were not content with just walking the horses around, and started running them hard, through the sagebrush.

We became bored with just ridding, so we started roping bales of hay, until it also became too easy.

The bales of hay were sitting ducks, not like wild animals or even cattle. When Ernie's parents were not around, we would practice roping the family's dairy cows. These were not steers or range beef cattle. The dairy cows were worth a lot of money, and a big part of Ernie's family income. It would not be a good thing, if one of the milking money machines was injured, from our pretend cowboyin' practices.

It was time for me to get a horse, but my dad had little interest in my sidetrack adventures versus his plans for me.

After all, I was the son of a Washington State sports legend, the heir apparent to greatness. I should become Big Bob's gift to the *gridiron Gods*.

To placate my misspent efforts to fill my time, until success on the football field would take over his thoughts, Dad gave into me, to a point. "Rick you have to have a job, if you want a horse."

After my eight-grade year was over, Dad used his influence to get me a summer job at a local grain company, filling storage bins with local harvested peas at $1.25 per hour.

I applied myself, working hard, not complaining, to earn the one thing keeping me from my dream.

By the end of the summer, I had my seed, (pea) money to buy my horse.

* * *

13

THE BARGIN HORSE... BUYER BEWARE

... Especially if your eyes our blinded by a deep seated yearnin' to fulfill a childhood dream.

Along with the fact, I was still a kid. After I had shown Dad my earnings I had stowed away from my summer job, my dad drove me around, checking out every lead about horses for sale.

Most of the candidates we saw where either broken down trail horses, old nags, or just not right.

I was looking for a certain type that I referred to as 'The Horse.' '

Dad would joke about 'The Horse,' when asked by Mom or their friends, about the progress of their search. Dad knew all too well about having your mind set on something, and the price you'd have to pay to achieve it.

To say that I was singled mind... was an understatement. Every time someone tried to change the subject or deflect me away from my passion with other projects or alternatives I stood my ground. That ground being where my new horse would be kept and how soon.

My Dad was patient, with his son's tunnel vision search to find...

'The Horse.'

* * *

14

FERGERSON RANCH

TWO WEEKS LATER: SOAP LAKE, WASHINGTON

I sat between, Nate Fergerson, a slim built man in his late sixties, driving, my dad in the front seat.

The Eastern Washington grasslands, outside the windshield, were bending in the gentle breeze.

We passed a sign on a split rail fence.

It read... FERGERSON RANCH - SELECT PALOMINOS FOR SALE...

"Thanks for your time Mr. Fergerson," I said.

"It's Nate. Nice to see a young man bit by the 'gotta have a horse bug'... right?"

I grinned at Nate and said, "Yes sir!"

"Hope it's not terminal. He has put everything on hold, including his grades, and sports," My dad said.

"I usually only have girls come by these days," Nate replied, his eyes fixed out of the windshield.

The miles rolled by outside.

"How large is your place sir?" I asked.

"Just shy of thirty thousand acres," he said.

"How many horses do you have?" I asked.

"Rick... enough questions," Dad said.

Nate laughed. "We have about a hundred head of good color Palominos. Only God knows for sure how many I've culled out to pasture."

"I just need one sir." I said.

Dad made eye contact with Nate, who pointed out the windshield. "There is my western wild herd," Nate said.

* * *

A little later, we arrived at the Fergerson Ranch. Nate's pickup was behind the ranch house. My Dad walked over and stood next to Nate Fergerson, who was leaning on a split rail fence. They looked out at the horses grazing a hundred yards away, on the grasslands.

I stared at the two men, with plaid shirts and jeans, leaning on the top of the fence rail. Their right boots were planted on the bottom rail, as if partners' in some grand scheme, happening soon.

Walking up to the men, I slid my boot on the bottom rail, next to my dad. Resting my left forearm on the top rail, I pointed with my right hand to a frisky sorrel colored horse, and said, "That's the one!"

"Are you sure son?" My dad asked.

I shrugged, giving my dad that...

'Are you kidding me?' look.

"He has been looking every day since he has been out of school. Probably several hundred different ones... at least," Dad said to Nate.

I climbed through the fence. The horses looked at the intruder. The frisky sorrel snorted my way.

"Whoa boy...you're going to spook them." Nate said.

"How much do you want for the sorrel with the white blaze, and one white sock?" Dad asked.

"Any horse out there... one hundred in my corral."

"How much if I bring in myself?" I asked, all puffed up, and about to explode.

Nate and dad smiled at each other.

"Now easy son..." Nate said.

"I can do it!" I said.

"Fifty will do."

"It's a deal," I said, inching towards the horses.

"We'll see how tough he really is," dad said to Nate.

I took a full step towards the horses. Several horses snorted, and then they all ran off into the distance.

*   *   *

15

COWBOY UP

SOAP LAKE WASHINGTON - FERGERSON RANCH

We returned the next day, for me to begin taming my new horse, or so I figured.

Dad pulled up and parked his State Patrol car next to the horse corral, in the back of the Fergerson Ranch House.

Ernie and I stepped out of the Ford Cruiser, both of us dressed in our finest cowboy outfits. We wore plaid shirts, Levis of course, dime store Stenson knock off hats, and bargain cowboys boots.

Nate Fergerson stood inside the coral, holding the reigns for two saddled up working horses.

I could see Mr. Fergerson felt sorry for me... a little. He let me and Ernie borrow a couple of his working saddle horses. I figured we would need the saddles only a day or two at the most.

Mr. Fergerson had tied on a bedroll, saddlebags with some cowboy trail chow, and two lariats on each saddle. Ernie and I added some treats to the saddlebags we intended to share, after roping the horse.

Mounting up on the horses, we let out shouts, while guiding the horses out of the corral.

"Boys it's about a two hour ride to get where the herd is. Try not to run the horses before you need too. Have fun." Nate said.

"We will. Thanks Mr... I mean Nate," I said, as Eddie and I waved goodbye.

* * *

"What do you think Nate?" Dad asked, as we topped the hill, about a mile away.

"Sometimes youthful expedience gives way to reality." Nate said.

"Like haste makes waste... look before you leap... stop and think. All are foreign to Rick." Dad said.

* * *

16

END OF ROUNDUP

SOAP LAKE WASHINGTON - FERGERSON RANCH –
FIVE DAYS LATER:

Dad's Patrol car was where we had last seen it, outside the horse corral.

Nate Fergerson stood next to the open gate to the horse corral, talking to my dad. He had called my dad to notify him that one of his wranglers had gone out to check on us, and found us leading a range horse back towards the ranch house. The wrangler guessed we would be back around midday... if the horse did not somehow escape.

Ernie and I came into their view, mounted on the horses Nate had lent to us. We were exhausted, filthy, riding ten feet apart. Separate ropes tied around our saddle horns, their free ends looped around the neck of an unhappy spirited wild gelding.

We zoned in on our goal, unable to acknowledge the men standing by the open gate. Inside the corral, the horse became uneasy, throwing his head up and down.

Nate closed the corral gate behind us, and walked over to where I had dismounted.

"Hand me your rope Rick," Nate said. After I unwrapped the rope off the saddle horn, Nate tied it fast to a fence post. Ernie started to untie his rope, but the horse stomped away tightening the rope, then breaking loose from Ernie's saddle horn.

Nate caught up with the loose rope and wrapped it around the same fence post.

Ernie dismounted, fell to the ground and yelled, "Thank God... it's over!"

The horse pulled hard on his tether, rearing up and snorting.

"Smooth move Ernie," I said.

Nate walked down the tied off ropes, whispering to the horse, and then patted the horse's neck. In a low voice, "It's ok boy... it's ok." He said.

The horse sensed the old man's kindness, and settled down. "Better go home and rest up son. He'll still be here tomorrow," Nate said. I started to protest then thought better of it.

"Rick... got a name for him yet?" Nate asked.

"Rego. Saw it somewhere, but not sure what it means," I said.

"Good name... short... easy to say to him."

"See you first thing tomorrow," I said, walking towards my dad's car.

Nate raised a hand and turned away.

* * *

17

BREAKIN' WHOM?

FERGERSON RANCH - NEXT MORNING

Ernie and I walked ahead of Rego, leading him by the reins, around the corral. Rego's saddle, blanket, and halter already in place.

A state patrol car rolled up to the corral. My Dad stepped out in his patrol uniform. He walked over to the corral fence, stepping onto the bottom rail.

Many of the non-horse people did the same thing, all wondering what it would be like to be in control of a wild animal. Like the ranch hands did, or the horse savvy people, just judging the action.

Dad made eye contact with me and asked... "You gonna break him now?"

"Rick...Do a couple more turns around the corral, and he'll be ready," Nate said.

"We've been doing this all morning," I protested.

"He needs to feel the weight more," Nate said. I pouted, but did as Nate had instructed me.

A couple of Mr. Fergerson's ranch hands stood on the bottom rail of the corral for a better look at the kid's ego education.

I couldn't breathe, my stomach raised in my throat, making it hard for me to swallow. Ernie held fast with the rope, around the horse's neck. Rego raised up, his nostrils flaring.

Nate stood next to Rego, pulling down on the saddle horn, giving me my best chance to mount up.

I stepped into the hanging metal stirrup, swung my leg high and mounted the horse... almost.

I grazed off the saddle horn with my crotch, before hitting the ground hard. A cloud of dust swirled towards the spectators.

"Hey kid... kinda like ridin' your bike in the dirt?" Nate joked, receiving roaring approval from the cowhands.

I rolled on the ground, came to my knees, spitting out a wad of saliva soaked dust. "More like trying to help my Ma put a load of my sister's dirty things into the washing machine," I said, to no one in particular, while trying to put on a brave face.

Nate grinned at Ernie and said, "Help the young man from Ephrata become one."

Ernie nodded at Nate, after my futile attempts to stay on the back of the wild animal, determined not to be ridden.

Ernie gladly helped the big shot kid to a half dozen more remounts.

For the next hour, I didn't quit, the horse didn't either. Sundown found both of us combatants weary from our ordeal. I dragged my sore body on the equally exhausted animal, one last time. Leaning forward, holding onto the panting horse's mane, I gave a nod for Ernie to release the beast. Sometimes even the most determined fools are rescued from themselves.

"Hey cowboy... chow time," Nate said, walking away. I slipped off the horse, not waiting for a second opinion from any of the peanut gallery hecklers, I quickly followed Nate.

* * *

18

UNBROKEN STILL

Breaking Rego at home:

I walked into our front yard, leading Rego by the reigns.

"Is he broke yet?" My sister, Gail asked.

I gave her an (*Are-you-really-asking-that?*) smirk. "Rode him yesterday... at old man Fergerson's."

"Are you sure?" she asked.

My over confidence on display, I blurted out... "I have a broke horse. It's time to start training him!"

I had put the saddle and reigns on the reluctant Rego, just minutes earlier.

Dad had helped me build a makeshift temporary ten-foot square corral the day before, in our back yard.

Getting Rego home from the Fergerson Ranch was entirely another matter.

* * *

A *Rube Goldberg* endeavor... like any of Goldberg's overly thought out inventions. A century old not-so-wise man.

His rule of limited success, *find a complicated way to do a simple task.* And we did.

Animal rights people would have tarred and feathered me, if that had been present when we loaded Rego into the horse trailer for the first time.

Dad had borrowed a homemade plywood sided horse trailer, from another State Patrol officer.

I lead Rego away from the Fergerson Ranch, to where dad had parked the horse trailer.

We were out of sight of the ranch house.

When I tried to walk Rego up the plywood ramp, into the topless homemade trailer, he reared up and refused to walk inside. We ran a rope through a hole in the trailer's front end. Dad pulled on the rope, and I swatted Rego's flank.

Rego just reared up and snorted. No way was he going to walk up the ramp into the trailer.

"Rick, make him lie down at the base of the ramp," Dad said. I managed to make Rego lie down on the bottom of the ramp. Dad tied the rope around Rego's neck, and to the saddle horn.

Dad unfastened the trailer from the pickup truck and blocked the tires with large rocks, to keep it from rolling forward.

With the free end of the rope tied to the truck's trailer hitch, Dad drove the truck away, dragging Rego on his side up the ramp, into the trailer.

Necessity is the mother of invention.

No injury to Rego, his horsehide provided the insulation needed, to hurt only his pride.

Loading Rego into a horse trailer once again, was a sudden movement of beauty. Even a stubborn animal can learn from such events.

* * *

My ego maxed out, both hands on the saddle horn, I stepped down into the stirrup and swung my right leg high over Rego's backside.

The primitive survival instinct fuse exploded in Rego's mind. *Get this darn dead weight off me!* If a horse could think like a human... Rego thought.

* * *

To say Rego just bucked me off was an understatement.

I could see over the top of our house. I could see Rego's corral in the back yard, I thought, reaching our house's stratosphere, fifteen feet or so above Rego's leather saddle launching pad.

Ground zero jarred all my senses. Even my sense of taste smelled of the toast my brain had become.

"Rick, are you okay?" Gail yelled.

My saving grace became the wet grass, after morning watering. Unable to answer my sister, I was still wandering around in la-la land.

Was I dreaming? Rego ran off into the distant grasslands, at the edge of our street.

I lost count of how many times Rego bucked, trying to free the rider-less saddle from his back.

* * *

19

HORSE SENSE VERSUS COMMON SENSE

I walked ahead, leading Rego into our backyard. Our property fronted on the alley, bordering the Ephrata water canal.

It had taken me only half an hour to track down Rego. He stood in the waist high sweet grass, munching away, just a quarter mile from the end of C Street. When I approached him, he acted as if nothing had happened between us.

A feedbag full of choice grains in my hand caught his eye. I had been using that trick earlier that morning to put the halter and bit on him.

Rego let me approach him and slip the feedbag onto his head. A nice treat he never attained while running wild in the grasslands of Eastern Washington.

I tied Rego's reigns to a fence post, on a small corral.

"Need to find a way big fella," I said to Rego.

* * *

I asked Nate for some advice. The next morning I started building the bucking shoot Nate had suggested to me.

I built the bucking shoot out of 2X4 and 2X6 wood boards. It measured twenty-feet long and just a little wider for a horse and rider to squeeze inside the shoot.

The wooden shoot's sides were five-feet high and there was a gate at both ends, to allow easy access for a horse.

Nate said I needed to get Rego used to strange noises and movements without bucking me off.

I started by saddling Rego, leading him into the bucking shoot and closing both gates trapping him inside.

Next, I climbed over the railing and sat in the saddle, while waving my coat over my head. At first, Rego tried to jump and stomp his hooves but soon tired of this tactic. At last, he became used to objects flashing by in his line of sight. The first step in what seemed like a thousand mile journey.

Another drill consisted of hitting Rego on his head and shoulders with a towel. Soon he just put up with the distractions.

After a week of repeated drills, I was able to back Rego out of the bucking shoot and walk him down the alley, behind my house.

Now I was able to ride him under my control. The only thing I could not do was make him run. This led to me setting the tumbleweed on fire behind me, and all of the issues that one decision created in my life.

* * *

20

THE GRAND CANYON JUMP

The last rays of summer twilight gave way at the Ephrata Riding Club, turning the large riding rink, into a somber circle of gray shadows.

That rink had been jumping with activity just minutes before, and now was patrolled only by a single mounted rider. Determined more than ever, I pushed Rego through his drills so that we could both be State Champions.

"Better give Rego and yourself a break. Can't improve if you two are both worn out!" Mrs. Gault, the stable manager, said.

I didn't want to stop, but knew she was right. My dad was not happy with my all day training Marathons.

I coaxed Rego out of the rink and onto the trail that led back toward our house.

"Nice day Rick... have a safe ride home," Mrs. Gault said.

"Thanks Mrs. Gault... I will."

Safe is a matter of opinion. To me, fast was the safe choice. With all the mass murderers that must be lurking out there for naive little children, in the wild grasslands of Eastern Washington. Haste was a prudent choice.

It sounded plausible to me, my excuse for going like crazy all the way home in the dark. A speeding bullet would be no match for a simpleminded child molester.

At least the moon came out bright, and Rego was already at full gallop. Another minute and I had him at all out flank speed. I loved the wind in my hair, my eyes watering. "Take us home boy," I yelled into the night wind.

I could just make out the fork in the trail. I nudged Rego to take the right fork, but he chose the left fork instead. We had never gone this way, but I just let Rego find his way home.

The pounding of Rego's hooves onto the firm, almost virgin soil, lulled me into relaxing...

What could go wrong? Rego and I were one with the trail. *What a ride I was having.*

The moonlight reflected off the tall sweet grass and patches of smooth barren ground. I closed my eyes and was sucked into a moment of bliss.

Tall tumbleweeds brushed my side, scraping my pant leg. I woke up to a huge black hole racing towards us.

Reaching up, I pulled back on Rego's reigns and hesitated... *'it's too late.'* I thought.

We were airborne. The only sound heard was my pounding heart. The black hole engulfed us. The only visible light came from the moon, over this empty space I traveled.

Something flashed up at us from below. Then, it too was lost to the darkness.

The ground grabbed Rego's rear hooves then his front pair, forcing me to lunge forward. Only quick action allowed me to hang onto Rego's neck and right my coming fall. A moment later, Rego had regained his normal stride. I pulled back on the reigns.

"Whooa!" I yelled.

And Rego did stop. I leaned over his back and caught my breath. After dismounting, I lead Rego back towards the hole.

I got down on my knees and peered over the edge of the hole. There was just enough light to make out large objects, on the bottom. One of them was unmistakable... an old rusty refrigerator. I was in shocked to see how large and deep the hole was. "Well boy... glad you had enough steam to carry our sorry butts over this mess," I said to Rego. He looked down and snorted back at me.

*   *   *

TALE OF THE TAPE:

My buddy Ralph and a girl named Chris, watched Ernie climb down the side of the big hole and hold the end of my dad's hundred-foot cloth measuring tape.

My dad had used the tape to check out our property lines. And when my dad wasn't looking I snuck his measuring tape out of the garage.

"Just over ten-feet deep," I read off the tape. "Ernie... climb up the other end of the hole, and we'll see how long she is."

Five minutes later, Ernie had made it up the far side of the hole, and held the tape's end on the holes edge. And just in front of Rego's hoof marks, from the day before.

"Thirty one feet on the nose," I said looking down at Rego's rear hoof mark, a foot from the hole's rim. "So the hole is right on thirty feet across... like I said this morning."

We all slid down into the hole, checking out the half dozen old appliances, scattered on the bottom. We found nothing of any value. A set of deep rutted tire tracks led away from the hole, towards C Street. The hole was where people ditched their unwanted pieces of junk.

Luckily, Rego got us across safe. A foot further and Rego would have been busted up... real good for sure.

He would have probably been put down, and not to mention me... I could have died for sure.

But what a ride! Best of my life! So far that is!

* * *

21

THE FAUX RATTLESNAKE TRICK

Before Ernie and I rounded up and tamed Rego, we would share riding privileges on his horse. Ernie's dad had landed a new job driving a log shaving truck, and moved his family into town.

Ernie moved his horse to the Saddle Club where we could both ride his horse. But that was before the horse got out one night, and was killed by a car, on the highway.

I lost my riding partner's horse. Then along came Rego. Relishing my new opportunity, and driven to make the best of it, I entered many horse competitions.

Every night, I would saddle up Rego, and ride up to the Saddle Club to practice. I always ran Rego both ways, to build up his and my stamina.

But after our encounter, with the big nasty hole from hades, I made sure we steered clear of another date with tragedy.

* * *

Afterwards, I started attending 4H events and horse shows, entering all that I possibility could.

One warm summer afternoon, found a dozen of us 4H-ers ridding our horses, and following our twenty-four-year-old team leader, Ms. Johnson's car.

She steered her car down Palisades Road, in the canyon of the same name, for fifteen miles, to the McCartney Creek camping spot.

After setting up our camp spot, we split into small groups of three or four riders, to check out the surrounding countryside. We were told to find interesting things to share with the group, at the nightly campfire meeting.

I had teamed up with three guys about my age; Ernie Johnson, Ralph Collier and Chuck Clayton. Ralph's horse started to rear up and snort at the sound of a startled big rattlesnake, just a few feet away, from the trail.

Always looking for some adventure, I motioned for the others to dismount and follow me. The rattler, sensing our numbers, decided to crawl away, instead of confronting us.

After tying our horse's reins off to some small tree trunks nearby, I picked up a forked dead tree branch, and pinned down the retreating rattler's head to the ground. The snake twisted its body wildly, trying to free itself.

"Hey Ernie, hand me your knife!" I yelled, as he held an open pocketknife in his hand.

Holding down the snake's head with the forked stick in my left hand, I ended the rattler's torment with a quick thrust of the pointed knife blade to the back of its head.

"Wow must be a six-footer!" Ernie said.

Holding the dead snake by the tail, high in the air, I said, "Five plus for sure." Emboldened by my manly achievement, I dropped the snake into my saddlebag. "I have a cool idea for the campfire meeting... let's go back."

*   *   *

When we got back for the evening, I made sure no one saw me. I coiled up the big rattler... propped up its head with a chunk of wood to the striking position... complete with its mouth pried open to bite, with a small stick inside, exposing its deadly fangs.

A real work of twisted art... I thought, at the time.

My masterpiece was located just feet away, from where we would all be sitting at the fire pit sharing our mundane tales of the daily adventures.

So much for a plan of genius.

A coiled up six-foot rattler would have made a loud, terrifying sound.

My silent creation, only a few feet away from where I sat next to sixteen-year-old Linda Lidke, went unnoticed by thirteen people, engrossed in storytelling for a half an hour.

The snake was less than two feet to the side, behind clueless Linda.

As we were about to break off for the night, I panicked, pointed to my prize and shouted out to the group...

"Oh my God, look at that big rattler!"

Linda jumped to her feet in terror, screaming as if the dead snake had bitten her, and ran off, into the dark night.

She crashed through brush like a wounded water buffalo. We all ran to find her, and calm her down.

Some of the guys thought my idea was cool. None of the gals, or Ms. Johnson, saw the humor in sending poor Linda to the Looney Farm, even for just a short visit.

Linda could not calm herself down. Ms. Johnson drove Linda back to her home that night, before coming back to our camp out.

We guided Linda's horse back to the stables in Ephrata, behind one of ours, when our camp out was over. We never went on an OVERNIGHTER again. Many years later, at our fifty-year class reunion, Linda said she had no memory of that day. This was not a highpoint of good deeds for me.

*   *   *

I entered the Grant County Fair Horse event, the Moses Lake event, the Quincy, The Omak stampede and the Okanogan, to name a few.

The Ephrata Saddle Club would be sending eight to a dozen teams of riders to each event.

The events consisted of Bareback, relay, and cowhide events.

They had eight categories; Poll Bending, Barrel Racing, Scurry, Flag race, Cowhide race, Bareback Relay, Western pleasure and Western actuations.

I entered all of them, and received ribbons in everything.

My teammate in the bareback relay was the heaviest girl in the club, to make it fair for the other club members.

I had to run down a slalom course, reach down pick up the girl and race back to the finish. But we still won, most of the time.

Later, my prize mount and I won the lion's share of the Pacific Northwest 4H horse riding events.

However, the big banana of horse events was the State Telegraphic Meet.

Four states held their State Championship events together in the same arena: The states of Oregon, Montana, Idaho and Washington, and was called 'The Jim Canyons.'

I won the Pole Bending event and was crowned the Champion of all four states. In that event, I ran Rego in the .slalom, around six polls, sticking out of the ground, and back to where I started.

In addition, I also became the Four State Champion in the Keyhole Race. Think of a balls-to-the wall full-out U-Turn on horseback. Running down the narrow shoot, I would yell "Whooa!" to Rego. He would start sliding sideways going into a U-turn back the way we came.

The race course had lines running down the sides, if you touched the line anywhere, you were assessed a five-second penalty. Rego and I ran clear... and our time was the best by far.

But my proudest moment was having my picture taken, with my mom and dad, with the Championship Grand Stands in the background.

*   *   *

22

THE WATER HORSE

Lizbula Resort, Vashon Island, Washington 1959, a retreat from everyday life.

My paternal grandparents paid for us to have a summer getaway on the Puget Sound, complete with a cabin and small rental fishing boat.

In the pic below, Dad holds baby Nancy. Mom sits in front. My sisters Harriet and Chris on the bow. My bud Ernie and I stand in the stern.

Dad stepped up to make it special, allowing us kids to take along a dog, a cat, a parakeet and, of course, my horse Rego.

Dad had to rewire a borrowed horse trailer that took less time to fix. Dad and I spent more time trying to get stubborn Rego into the trailer. Just after midnight, and after several failed attempts to drag him in, I had to mount up on him, using my spurs, to coax him inside the trailer.

There we were in the pitch black of night, finally on our way in our 56 Ford station wagon loaded to the max... with nine humans, one snarling kitty, one panting dog and one chirping bird, on a hot and sweaty five-hour drive. Not the thing of storybook memories.

All our belongings were either loaded onto the car's roof rack, or crammed into every nook and cranny of the station wagon's interior. It was as if we were the old T.V. show's Hillbillies, Jed and Ma Clampton, with their young'un's.

The difference, we weren't moving to Beverly Hills, but to the Puget Sound south of Seattle.

The sunrise found us finally pulling into the Resort's parking spot, next to our rental cabin. I made another bonehead move, after we moved into the cabin and had eaten breakfast.

Because there was no room to bring any fencing material to build a corral for Rego, I had brought along some clothesline cording material. I figured I could use standing tree trunks, and the side of the horse trailer as a fence post, to make a makeshift corral, by arranging the clothesline into a small square enclosure. With one clothes line tied in at a horse's knee level and a second line at Rego's chest height.

All I had to do was lead Rego into the enclosure, by walking him over one of the clothesline ends, lying on the ground. Once he was inside, I would tie them up high.

Pretty cool huh? Duh!

My corral worked for the first day, because Rego was tired from the long ride in the horse trailer. The next day, when we were boating, he saw what a poor job I had done.

The lines on one end of the corral were sagging, but still tied off. I figured that Rago had simply stepped over the lower line, and ducked his head, while walking under the upper one. He was nowhere in sight. We spent the next several hours driving up and down, looking for my escaped horse to no avail. There were two saddle clubs down the road and lots of buildings with people all around, but he had just evaporated into thin air.

Then, a couple of fishermen pulled up in a small boat, saw the commotion. One of them asked, "Are you folks looking for a horse?"

I ran up to them and said, "Yeah, mister... have you seen a sorrel with a white blazed face?"

"Don't know about the color... but we saw a horse about a mile out swimming like he was trying out for the swim team."

Ernie and I jumped into our rental boat and headed out to sea, looking for my horse. Just like the fisherman said, Rego was swimming like a champ a mile out from shore, in the Puget Sound.

I roped him just like the first time with my rope around his neck and led him behind the boat, back to shore.

He was no worse for the wear from his ordeal, and settled back into a repaired corral. I borrowed some lumber, and made his temporary home more secure this time. Rego must be part Labrador Retriever, as I have never seen a horse that loved the water and loved to swim more that he did.

*   *   *

23

MY CANAL WATER-SKI TEAM

THE GREAT GRANDMOTHER OF INVENTIONS:

What do bored Ephrata, Washington young lads, with an access to a car, do on a very hot summer day?

What fun to go water skiing on a hot summer day?

And even better without a boat.

The first time I saw guys slalom water ski down the canal, behind a car, blew my mind.

I had to try it for myself.

Thanks to *The Columbia Basin Project*, the irrigation network that the Grand Coulee Dam made for us to exploit. The largest water reclamation project in the United States. Water pumped from the Columbia River is carried over 300 miles of main canals, stored in a number of reservoirs, then fed into over a thousand miles of lateral irrigation canals.

And there was one in our backyard, literally behind my house. I talked a buddy into driving down the gravel service road fronting the canal with me hanging onto a ski rope tied to his bumper.

The concept was simple for simple-minded young fools.

The car was parked parallel to the canal, a ski rope tied to its rear bumper. I slid into the canal wearing my cutoff jeans and yelled to my buds.

Someone tossed me the skier's end of the rope. I pushed off from the bank, and slipped on my water skis. I waited for the car driver to inch forward enough to take the slack out of the ski rope.

I gave him thumbs up. The driver floored the car, and off he went, up I popped swerving back and forth on my single salmon ski.

Later, when I gave the other guys a run at the fun, a couple of them got a little skinned up from the concrete canal lining, when they climbed in and out of the water.

But It was a small price to pay for a day of fun.

What a rush!

* * *

24

THE OTHER T-BONE - NOT THE STEAK!

In the summer of 1959, I was not thinking of my upcoming junior year of high school.

Instead, I was thinking of girls!

My high school buddy, Jim Brengle, was a wana-be 'Ladies Man.'

Jim and I met two very attractive young women, from Western Washington. They were visiting our little burb with some friends.

We spent some time getting to know them. One of them said they wanted to see the Grand Coulee Dam.

I suggested we could take them to see the Dam, and then take them home to Maltby, Washington.

Grand Coulee Dam was not exactly on the way to their homes, north of Seattle, only 300 hundred miles east, and a 4-hour drive each way.

Young and foolish we were in spades. Both of us had little cash, but huge ideas... if you get my drift.

The long drive rewarded us, with little time to do ANYTHING else.

The result of our adventure would mimic a maneuver I would master years later, on the airplane runway of the military flight school with a T-28 flight trainer aircraft, in Florida. We did a *touch-and-go*, at the Grand Coulee Dam,

Instead of the airplane takeoff into the cool wild blue yonder. we turned the car around, retracing the long hot highway, back through Ephrata. Hours later, we dropped the girls off, in Maltby, at five in the morning.

We had only gone a few miles when Jim's '54 Ford ran out of gas. The good news... we were on top of a hill, parked next to the curb.

Our weary bones could go no further.

Jim climbed into the back, and I stretched out in the front seat. We got some needed shuteye.

Later that morning, a car swishing by us outside, woke me up. I thought I saw what looked like a gas station down the hill, in the distance.

I put the car in neutral and released the emergency brake. Opening the driver's door, I stepped outside, gave the car a push, before jumping back inside.

Lucky for us, the hill was steep and we were moving at a good clip, until we ran a stop sign, at the bottom of the hill, and rolled across a busy four-lane highway.

We almost coasted through. I mean, I did. Jim did not.

An Oldsmobile station wagon T-boned hard into the Ford's rear quarter panel, where Jim sat.

So far, I had struck out on life. I mean the numbers really didn't add up for me. But I could still walk away from this mess, I engineered.

Poor Jimbo broke an arm, and was taken to the hospital. I was unhurt at the first. At least physically.

My dad was mad as hell... to start with.

Mom and he were away visiting family. And I was told NOT to leave the yard, and to be sure and water it.

Jim's car was a totaled, because of me. Strike one. I left the house. Strike two. But I did water the yard real good, ball one. Actually a little too good.

I left the water running for three days. Two days after Dad got home, he went down to our basement and found three feet of standing water. Strike three... out at home!

* * *

25

LAYING THE WOOD... ON MY KEISTER

The start of my junior high year, in 1959, had been interesting. Dad was still wishing I would get the football bug. One day maybe, but right now I was still into youthful shenanigans.

After school, I had some time to kill before heading home. I went to the horse stables... to see what was happening.

My pal Ralph had just gotten a new horse. He was tied up outside the horse barn. After checking the corral areas, I found that there wasn't anybody around.

Where is everybody and why is Ralph's horse tied to the barn, I wondered.

A stray dog, that I did not recognize, or whom it belonged to, came running up to me. I stared at the dog and it took off running.

Go figure, I thought.

I returned to Ralph's horse and started checking it out to see if it was a runner.

The dog came back with a vengeance, barking and dancing around.

Ralph's horse spooked, jerking on the rope that tied him to the barn.

I tried to steady the horse, as he jerked back busting off the 2X4 it was tied to. The board slammed into me hard, knocking me to the ground, in a pile of sure pain.

Time stood still. Then my arm was on fire with pain. I tried to roll over, but cried out, clasping my side with my only good arm.

Time drug on... no one came. I just laid there in too much pain to care.

Three hours later, I lay in a hospital bed, with a broken arm and cracked ribs. An injured warrior of such, but not the gridiron my Dad would have been proud of.

I had become a wounded horseman, because of a stupid dog. Not from being thrown off a splendid racehorse, while going like hell across the grasslands of Washington State.

Sad... real sad. What a waste. *I could never live this down. Grounded by a stray dog!*

* * *

PART THREE
WSU

Become a man... set aside childish things
Maybe not just yet???

26

HONOR THY FATHER

Bob Grimstead was proud that his only son would soon follow in his footsteps. Kind of... but not really.

Bob Grimstead, in 1936, was everything in all sports in high school and at WSU. I enrolled at WSU, pledged to join and was accepted to Delta Tau Delta fraternity. The kind of thing like dad had done... the frat wise thing.

But I was never going to be the jock... big Bob was.

The frat was not a jock or geek house, closer to John Belushi's *Animal House,* but not as whacko. They had obtainable real world standards, if you tried a little to conform.

So much for the honor part...just over two weeks later, after settling into my fraternity, I was ceremonial ordered to move my ass out. Something real lame about mischievous conduct, or at best... a simple misunderstanding.

I sat on the sidewalk, outside Delta Tau Delta. I looked like Tom Hanks... in the movie *'Castaway,'* staring off into the endless ocean swells, waiting to be rescued.

I was a man on an island all right, an island of shame. Except I never seemed to give a shit what others thought. The fraternity was the next closest building to the main campus, just a block from the library, and all the student traffic.

I watched the people flooding by me, looking at my suitcase and desk lamp lying next to the curb.

"Looks like you're looking for a roommate?" Johnny Crapner asked, stopping for a reply.

"For sure?"

Johnny nodded and said, "I'm on the second floor." He pointed to the dormitory building between the frat house, and the library.

Just another time I made lemonade out of lemons, or better yet, expelled from a life of rules and regulations, to a life of party hearty. And closer to school... if only by just one building.

In less than fifteen minutes, I moved in with Johnny, and resumed my quest to better myself.

My roommate, Johnny Crapner, turned out to be more like the first four letters of his last name... but the price was right.

I made the best of it, filling out the rest of the school year learning the ways of all the young ladies, on their way to the library to study.

And study... I did. Not many opportunities escaped my diligent attention for the coeds in need of some assistance.

*   *   *

27

EVER PATH HAS ITS PUDDLE

... or a Great Salt Lake to cross.

In my freshman year at Washington State University, with marginal effort, I attained about a 2.0 'C' grade point average. I decided to actually study and apply myself, netting straight A's in all my classes to mid-term, in my sophomore year.

My downfall was when I learned that half my grade for the semester would be based on what I had already obtained. The other half on the remaining daily work, until the end of the school year.

To me a 'C' average in my classes, was all I really wanted.

So I came up with a brilliant plan to add goof-off time to my life. I would not attend any classes.

In October, I bought a season ski pass at White Pass Ski Resort, to sharpen my downhill racing skills.

Anyone seeking immediate gratification from daily activities, would see my brilliant plan made perfect sense.

I figured if they averaged the A's I already had on my midterms, with the F's I would get for not attending regular classes, I would still net solid C's, and all would be wonderful.

My half-ass plan...equaled and smelled liked a similar result, born from the hole sandwiched between my butt cheeks.

The problem was… a grade of 'A' was equal to about a 92% score level. Add the 92% to the 0% I got for not showing up, you get an average of 46%. In most school classes, it takes about a 70% average to achieve a minimum 'D' grade level.

So I got straight F's for my not so incandescent, screw off, dumb shit idea.

I was still living on campus, to throw my dad off, to any of my extra curriculum activities.

I was oblivious to my grades report from hell, which was ready to be mailed to my home in Ephrata and I was much too busy preparing myself for WSU's on campus Spring Break Shenanigans.

Delta Tau Delta held their Scholarship Dinner, followed by the Sally Sunshine Contest where my latest girlfriend Yvonne LaCrouix won.

It was a little payback from a former frat brother, in a twisted sort of way.

*   *   *

28

ONE PRANK TOO FAR

DUMBER THING ONE:

"Hell! It's spring break... lets do something fun!" I said to Dan Radecki and Gary King, my partners in crime. "Let's go and show Queen Sally Sunshine a little respect."

* * *

The three dorm-a-tiers' plan was to stage a Greek battle pageant for the Queen's liking.

Complete with cheesy looking period costumes, swords made of wood, and best of all, metal trash can lids for shields.

We climbed up the metal fire escape, on the backside of the dormitory, making a lot of racket.

The occupant of the ground floor room, closest to the fire escape, looked out her window. She saw three male refugees from God knows what kind of a stage play, rucking it up, ascending the fire escape ladder.

Yvonne told me how she was crowned Sally Sunshine in a simple ceremony, at the Delta Tau Delta, following their Scholarship dinner. I envisioned a neat way to show her how much cooler I was, than my former frat brothers.

It would be something like Robin Hood and my Merry Men, rescuing Maid Marion from the evil King, with a Greek warrior slant.

But it was not in my plan... we three brutes entered Yvonne's dorm room, from the fire escape, tearing the curtains as we entered.

In addition, Dan and Gary fighting a mock sword battle, knocked over and broke not one, but two table lamps.

A rush of co-eds pushed their way into the dorm room, for a better look. Now, the first surprised smiling face of Yvonne morphed into a red faced, unhappy camper.

I had thought the happy Yvonne, and several of her roommates would follow the boys down the fire escape to party, in the street below.

Dan and Gary climbed back onto the fire escape. I faced the open window to climb out, motioning for the girls to follow them when...

"Ok... you guys come out with your hands where we can see them," blared over a loud megaphone, outside the dorm window.

The lights below were blinding. Three campus police officers, pointed spotlights at the three cat burglars, second-story men, or just dumb shits.

When we reach the ground, the police officers walked up to us. I recognized the lead officer. "Mr. Knickerman?"

"Richard Grimstead?" Mr. Knickerman asked back, shaking his head and grinning. "You boys are in a pile of trouble. What in the world were you boys doing?"

"We were just having fun with my girlfriend," I said. Mr. Knickerman was not impressed at my lame explanation.

Therefore, I tried to be more convincing, "She just won the Miss Sally Sunshine Contest and we were giving her a surprise celebration."

"The house mother is real upset... she wants me to charge you three with breaking and entering." Mr. Knickerman let that sink into our thick skulls. "It was her window on the first floor you clowns clanged by on your way up the fire escape."

"We kept our clothes on and everything. Just a little ceremony... no harm no fouls!" I said, smiling at my former high school teacher. I could tell he was having none of it, and my time before with him, had no influence this time.

He had moved on to better things, I guess.

Mr. Knickerman had quit his English teacher position, at Ephrata high school last year. He being a former WSU grad, secured the head of campus police job.

WSU alumni were thick as thieves, and looked out for each other like aliens from a far off world, protecting their own. We were all sons of grads. That alone cut us some slack, for at least one screw up.

"Since you boys haven't had any other run-ins with the law, I'm going to cut you a break," Mr. Knickerman said, glancing at each of us. "You each get a ticket for vagrancy... a ten dollar fine."

"Thanks Mr. Knickerman," I said.

"Boys... next time be smarter."

I knew my stupid actions... like embarrassing, Yvonne, in front of all her friends, burned a bridge with her.

What the heck... there are over 7,000 coeds enrolled at WSU. I have many more bridges yet to cross. I thought.

* * *

29

DUMBER THING TWO

Wednesday afternoon:

Dan and a couple other boys were complaining about how only fraternities had the girls in the dorms serenade them.

The custom was a frat boy would steal something belonging to one of the girls living in the dorms. The offended co-ed would have to bring along some girlfriends, stand outside the frat house, and serenade the frat boys to get her belongings back.

This was the perfect catalyst to get over my two-day-old heartbreak, of losing Sally Sunshine's favor.

It was simply a numbers game to me. With lots of cute co-eds to work my magic on since, I was an unknown person to them, like a fish out of water, in reverse.

Unlike my small high school, where everybody knew everybody's business, college offered me many opportunities to try out new things, on new people.

My next challenge was Roxanne. She lived in the Scott Hall dormitory, and had a much better sense of humor than my former squeeze. The Miss *'I'm not ready to let the good times roll, a little.'*

All of the guys were right. It was time to reap some of the fraternity benefits.

Dan followed me inside the front door of the Scott Hall dorm. Nobody was in the main gathering room.

I knew Roxanne's room was on the first floor, close to the main room.

I spotted a large potted plant in the hallway, next to a closed dorm room door.

"I think this is Roxanne's room," I said to Dan. "This is probably her plant...it's too big to be in her room."

Dan held the Scott Hall's front door open, as I slid the heavy plant through the doorway.

The two daytime bandits we had become, made off with our prize, loading it into the open trunk of Dan's car parked at the curb.

Desperadoes we were... speeding off and sharing laughs at our good fortune.

Later that afternoon, I sat at my desk, facing the open window. The large stolen plant stood on the small room's floor, crowded in between the dorm door and my backside.

Fast at it, composing some very important paperwork, I concentrated on my task.

A knock came at the door. "Yeah," I hollered, not turning to see whom it was, "Come in."

A man came through the door and stopped, staring at the huge, out of place vegetation.

"What are you doing Rick?" The voice asked.

"Oh... just changing my driver's license."

"Well, that's kind of illegal isn't?"

"Yeah right... who gives a shit? We're goin' drinking in Moscow tomorrow night."

"Yeah... Rick you haven't seen any potted plant have you?"

A red light turned on in my preoccupied brain. I did a slow one-eighty, turning to see the source of the question.

Through the plant's hanging leaves, stood Mr. Knickerman, with his eyes blazed on his former English student.

It had been only two days since my last run-in with the law. Now I was involved in two more separate crime issues.

The first was my paper copy of my Washington State driver's license, that I had a buddy make for me, at the college bookstore.

No big deal, everybody did it.

Well, almost everybody that needed to alter the date of their birth certificate, or driver's license, so they could go drinking across the state line, in Moscow, Idaho.

WSU is located in Pullman Washington, just eight miles from Idaho, and its lower minimum drinking age law.

The second little FOOPA (or a thoughtless stupid idea), the great potted plant heist was ground zero this time. The altered license was more of an issue in Idaho, since on this side of the border, store clerks demanded to see the real thing, not a paper copy.

"Holy smokes Mr. Knickerman...what are you doing here?"

Mr. Knickerman diverted his stare to the potted plant, running a leaf through two fingers. "The Scott Hall house mother wants me to charge the perpetrator with grand theft... a felony."

"The girls were going to come by and serenade our dorm... like they do for the frats, when they hold an item of one of the girls for ransom." I swallowed hard, knowing the mile deep hole I was digging for myself. "They're coming by tomorrow... we are going to give it back to them... we had no intention of ever keeping it."

"The plant belongs to the house mother... her dad paid over four hundred bucks for it... a birthday present."

I rubbed my head with both palms, letting out a breath, held in way to long.

"Last time cowboy... take the plant back right now... apologize to the house mother. You get another ticket. This one I'll write up as destruction of property... a misdemeanor.

*   *   *

30

DUMBER THING THREE

Friday noon: coupe de gras (A finishing stroke or decisive event) It was hot!

All the guys in my dorm decided it would be great fun to have water balloon fights, with the coeds at the sorority, located just down the hill, from our building.

Both sides of the battle, the men in cutoff jeans and swimming trunks, the ladies in revealing two-piece swim wear, tossed dozens of bright colored water filled balloons, towards each other.

Some of the fun balls of water finding their marks, some bursting open on whatever hard object they came across.

It was lots of harmless fun... until another brainstorm...

AKA another stupid brainfart of mine.

I retrieved a large pipe wrench from our dorm's maintenance room. Then I pranced over and opened the fire hydrant, located on the street, uphill from the women's sorority.

At first, everyone frolicked in the river of water, rushing down the street.

Some of the guys slid down the giant water slide the torrent of water had created, on the now wet grass hill, leading from the street to the sorority.

Mr. Knickerman walked up to me and my pals, as the Pullman Fire department closed off the gushing fire hydrant.

The futility of dealing with me finally came home to Mr. Knickerman. I shook my head, not saying anything, and he handed me my third ticket that week.

This ticket was for destruction of property... public and private.

The sorority suffered, what the ticket described as, minor flooding. I got my day in court. My dad called in some favors from the judge, and got my fines lowered from seven hundred to one hundred dollars and probation.

However, if my Dad had known about my flunking out of school, no telling how this would have turned out.

I figured I'd lived to fight another day. When Dad asked me to see my grades, I told him they haven't arrived yet. The truth... I had thrown the grades notice out, to buy some time. After two weeks of no grades, Dad drove his state patrol car to Pullman, and got the bad news from dean of students.

I had flunked out and my Dad's prodigal son was Summa Non-Grata to the entire WSU campus.

* * *

31

CAREFUL WHO YOU BEFRIEND

The summer of nineteen sixty-three in Eastern Washington State was hotter than usual.

Maybe the heat wave was because of some atmospheric condition. Maybe it was because of my Dad's attitude, about me being drummed out of WSU, even for just a few minor screw-ups, of all things.

Whatever... I promised my dad for the umpteenth time, "I got it figured out now... I'll get a job... make something of myself."

The job was in Plummer, Idaho. Paul Walk had just graduated from Ephrata High, and was one of the underclassmen that thought I was a cool guy in class.

When I told him about the summer jobs available at the Idaho Sand and Gravel Company, Paul jumped at the chance to share expenses with an old high school buddy.

I hitched my '46 Desoto repair project behind a '55 Chrysler, which Paul had picked up from the auto shop, complete with a hot new engine, tires and special wheels.

We took our sweet time driving the one hundred and fifty miles to drop off my car, in Lewiston, Idaho.

Amazing how thirsty a person can get with hundred plus degree winds, filling into the shiny metal box on wheels. We stopped along the way to sight see, to go swimming, or to relieve ourselves, because of all the liquids taken in to cool off.

Night surrounded us, when Lewiston, Idaho's city limit sign displayed into the Chrysler's headlights.

A friend of my Dads let me drop off my car for a couple days... until I would need it for the drive north, to my job in Plummer, Idaho.

We were now re-hydrated and free of my Desoto anchor. We headed the big Chrysler north, on Idaho highway 95, keeping our eyes open for some new adventure.

*   *   *

32

AMATUER TIME

... Not a bad thing!

Our goal was to get to the Lake Coeur d'Alene boat races, but it was still many miles of twisting mountain roads away.

Sensing the prize was just ahead, if only in our hopeful young minds, we half-assed sang along to *Blowing in the Wind,* by Peter Paul and Mary.

Time crept by. It was two in the morning, and the only radio station reception we had was the outlaw AM station in Del Rio, Texas.

The cult like king of late night radio, Wolfman Jack, who would be elected to the Radio Hall of Fame in 1996, barked out in his raspy voice...

"We are put on this earth to have a good time. This makes other people feel good...

And the cycle continues."

"That guy's nuts," Paul said.

"Sounds right to me." I replied.

Paul grinned, pushing the accelerator down a little harder, as Wolfman keyed up...

Fools Rush in where Angles Fear to Tread, by Rick Nelson.

"That's more like it... we ain't no fools though." Paul said.

I took a swig from my beverage bottle and said... "Nice corner... see how fast you can do the next one."

"Under control Rick... under control," Paul grinned back at me.

The yellow slow to forty sign, showing a curved arrow, illuminated.

Paul and I watched the speedometer needle dance on the fifty miles per hour mark. "I'll do better on this next one." Paul said.

The highway did not make us wait long.

Our next sign showed slow to forty-five. Paul skidded sideways, but made it around the curve at sixty. "Great job lct me try."

Paul pulled over, and we found our way around, the idling tank of a car in the dark night to the other sides.

* * *

33

EJECTED FROM THUNDER ROAD

... or balls larger than reality.

As I took over, steering the big car back onto the pavement, Wolfman's deep base voice came on again.

"Give us something to drive faster," I said. I sensed Paul was a little hesitant.

"Maybe you folks out there wonder how come our signal comes across so clear, all over the Western United States... one word describes our deal with the folks watching our transmitters, just across the border in Mexico," Wolfman Jack said, waiting for his audience to wonder...

Then, as only he could roll out said, "Mordida... a little mordida here. A little mordida there!"

Paul laughed, "Bribes."

"What?"

"Mordida in Spanish slang means to bribe."

"How the hell do you know that?" I asked.

"I paid attention in Spanish class. And you?"

I smirked back at my know-it-all wise-ass buddy.

"The word "mordida" literally means bite, but in Mexican slang it is used to mean a bribe, usually one paid to a public official." Paul said, loving his knowledge of trivia.

"Then bite me smart guy," I said, seeing the need to regain the moment.

The next sign showed... slow to 25mph.

My eyes lit up, at my chance to show off.

"Bet I can take it at sixty."

"You're crazy," Paul said, letting out a breath, squirming in his seat.

"Better not."

I reached over, turning up the radio.

Johnny Cash belted out *Ring of Fire.*

* * *

The sharp curve came on to us a little quicker than I had anticipated.

I turned the steering wheel sharp to the left. The Chrysler's front tires broke free on loose gravel, kicked onto the highway by previous vehicles also going too fast.

The big car did not follow my intended path, but continued straight ahead, lifting free from mother earth.

Johnny Cash sang out on the radio...

"I went down, down, down and the flames went higher. And it burns, burns, burns... the ring of fire... the ring of fire."

"Boy, the radio sure sounds great, without all the road noise," I said, glimpsing a quick look at Paul, who had a look of disbelief on his face.

Both of Paul's hands were digging into the dashboard. He was hanging on for his life.

Besides the crystal clear music, the only other sound was the engine's RPM increasing, from the lack of any road traction.

The big Chrysler reached its zenith of flight.

The three-ton monster started to come back to earth, both of us became weightless, for an instant.

I had a death grip on the steering wheel, while Paul flayed his arms like a mad man, looking for an invisible skyhook.

The steep downward embankment, allowed the car to first nosedive into the crushed rock road shoulder, before rolling over several agonizing times.

A loud crescendo of broken glass and smashing metal echoed off the steep canyon walls.

Johnny Cash's voice was no more.

The screaming whistles of escaping hot steam morphed into an eerie silence...

A radiance from the full moon reflected off the sea of broken glass, surrounding the remains of the Chrysler.

The sparkle from the countless stars, in the Pacific Northwest high desert sky, mirrored the counterfeit diamond display on the ground.

Wolfman's words still echoed in my mind.

"We are put on this earth to have a good time. This makes other people feel good...

And the cycle continues."

I didn't feel good... and Paul? Could he still feel anything? Anything at all?

*   *   *

34

LAZARUS CAN YOU HEAR ME?

My left hand gripped the steering wheel, as if clinging to the railing of Titanic's last life raft. The warm breeze biting at my swollen bloody right forearm drew my attention away from the moon shining through the hole that once held the windshield.

What in the hell happened, I thought?

I pushed the driver's door half way open grinding it to a stop against the rocky ground.

Rolling to my left, I plopped face first into the dirt. After coming to my knees, I grimaced.

I started pulling shards of broken glass out of my right hand and elbow.

The good news, the Chrysler had come to a rest on the right side up.

The bad news, gone was the engine, transmission, all the windows, all four wheels, and the hardtop had a terminal case of metal cellulite.

Paul was on his back only five-feet from the wreck, with his eyes shut. His white trousers and tee shirt were soaked in blood as dark as the crimson on the WSU school flag.

"Paul are you okay?" I yelled.

Oh, my God! He's dead. I thought.

Looking over at my friend, I hollered again. "Paul! Paul!"

There was no reply from Paul.

The warm desert breeze picked up its assault on my dry throat, as I tried to think.

What now? *Look at all these broken beer bottles on the ground.* *This must be where the Rez tribe toss their empties.*

I'd better pick them up, just incase.

Forty-five minutes later, I finished burying the last of the broken glass, in the sand wash.

I had been on a mission, like an inspector, in a NASA clean room.

Every bit of glass, no matter the color, the shape, within or close to the wreck I buried, under lots of sand and gravel.

I climbed up the embankment to where I thought Paul was lying dead.

* * *

35

WHISKEY ANGELS COMETH

A small chuckle, increasing to outright laughter and coming out from the corpse, made me freeze in my tracks.

"Dead men tell no tales. What's with burying all that broken glass?"

"You're alive... thank God! You looked deader than horse shit... flat on your back... not moving or saying anything." I said. I ran over to Paul, and dropped down to my knees, beside him.

"You could have checked."

"I could see you were dead, if not in this world, some other world."

Paul laughed again, "A little scary huh? So why bury all the glass?"

"Better safe, than sorry."

"Like sorry you took that corner so fast?"

"We need to get you to the hospital buddy!" I said, changing the subject.

I grabbed the now moaning Paul around his shoulders, pulling him up the steep slope, to the highway shoulder.

Trying to make sure I did not do any more damage to his ravaged body, I turned toward the highway.

I raised my arms like I was signaling for a touchdown, in a football game. The first set of oncoming headlights blew by me, into the distance, without even a hint of slowing down.

"Well there goes the first one Paul... must be in a hurry to get somewhere."

Fifteen minutes later, the next car slowed for an instant, then accelerated into the night.

"Not very trusting folks in these parts," I said, glancing to look at my buddy.

"Maybe I should lie down across the center line." I joked.

"The second dumbest thing you've come up with tonight," Paul said, starting to feel the pain from his injuries.

"I think we're in luck. This next guy is either moving real slow, or running out of gas." I said, waving my arms as the vehicle slowed to a stop, alongside us.

"Yeah maybe," Paul said, in a weak voice.

Two longhaired men sat in the darkened interior, of the old beat up Model A Ford pickup.

The truck's rusty paint job looked eggshell fragile. The smell of cheap booze wharfing out the open side window, confirmed my opinion of our two potential saviors... 'Reservation drunks!'

Beggars can never be too choosy. I remembered some bright guy asking me, when I needed a hand out.

"You chaps... need some help?" The driver asked.

"My buddy is in a world of hurt..." I said. "Can you fellows give us a lift to the hospital?"

"We don't got much gas," The truck's driver said.

"On our way back to the Rez...burp...sorry guys." The passenger said. I looked at Paul, turned, putting my hands on the driver's doorsill, and started to talk.

The driver interrupted me, "We passed a farm house, two miles back. Climb in the back, and we'll take ya there." He said.

The passenger and I helped Paul drag himself into what remained of the truck's decaying cargo bed.

*   *   *

36

THE GOOD FARM-ATARIAN

Ten minutes later:

I watched our rescuers swerve away, down the quarter mile long dirt driveway, from the farmhouse.

The Model A turned north on Idaho highway 95, heading for its home at the Coeur d'Alene Indian Reservation

Paul sat on the ground leaning against the trunk of a large oak tree, in the farmhouse's front yard.

I walked up the front steps to the dark house. It was three o'clock in the morning.

Thoughts of a pissed off redneck type, coming out and at this un-Godly hour with a vengeance on his mind, crossed my knuckle head. Had I created another mess with no way out?

I tapped on the screen door. First softly, then a couple louder knocks.

The farmhouse owner didn't come out with a shotgun blazing. He was the local reverend, and owned a station wagon.

Instead of hearing, "You two no good outlaws... don't move, or I'll blow you both to smithereens!" I heard the preacher say, "Oh my goodness, let me take you two boys to Saint Maries!"

* * *

37

A HOSPITAL WAS NO COUNTRY FOR A STUPID... YOUNG MAN

Our second bit of good luck: The first being we bad boys were still alive, and now we were in the waiting room of Saint Maries, Idaho General Hospital, just an hour and half later.

"Just a few pain killers, a band-aid or two, and we'll be fine." My words didn't go over well, with the two tired night nurses, on duty.

It seems some nurses have little patience for careless, young men these days.

Both of us road warriors waited in hospital beds. The nurses had patched us up pretty good, making sure we were out of danger, until the doctor came back on duty, later that morning.

I had scraped my right hand to the bone, when I busted out the windshield.

With my hand wrapped with gauze, and pain pills taking away some of the pain, I slipped out of bed.

"Lets go Paul... it's seven thirty. We can still make the boat races, in Coeur d'Alene, if we get going."

"I'm still pretty sore." Paul said.

"I saw where the nurse got the pain meds... I'll grab a couple more, on the way out." I said.

We slipped down the hallway, after another patient had distracted the nurses.

Paul could not support his own weight. He had to lean on me, as we reached the outside doors.

"Where in the heck are you two going?" The head nurse yelled.

"Boat races... we'll be okay." I said.

Both nurses raced to the doors, baring our bad boy getaway.

"You're not going anywhere, until the doctor checks you both out... period." The head nurse said.

"But..."

"No buts... get your butts back into bed!"

Paul let out a breath of relief, as the nurses' put him into a wheel chair. I followed them back into the exam room, tail between my legs.

Later that day, after the doctor checked us out, they transferred Paul to the Ephrata Washington Hospital.

Paul had a broken back, busted ribs, and internal injuries. He was lucky to be alive. Some buddy I was.

The hospital staff released me that afternoon. I had two wounds, a scraped hand, and a bruised ego.

As the ambulance had driven away with Paul inside, I wasted no time sticking out my thumb, bumming a ride with a trucker, going towards the Lake Coeur d'Alene boat races.

Why waste a hot summer day because of a little mishap? I thought to myself, while sitting next to the driver, weighing my good luck.

* * *

38

IF YOU DON'T REMEMBER YOUR MISTAKES

... you're doomed to repeat them... probably more than once.

After the truck driver dropped me off, I hitchhiked back to Lewiston, Idaho, retrieving my '46 De Soto, where I had dropped it off, two days before.

I thanked my Dad's friend for the favor, and started driving north on highway 95 again. Soon, I started going over the events in my mind, leading up to the accident.

I felt sorry for Paul for having to miss all the fun, at the boat races. I even felt a little responsible for the car crash.

Kind of... maybe a little... but really not.

Paul did start the horsing around first.

It wasn't my fault that Paul's car couldn't handle a little downhill, twenty-five miles per hour corner, at barely over sixty miles per hour. *Everyone knows the State puts up those signs for old people, chickens, and sissies.*

Come on... that tank of a car just did NOT cut it. Paul needed to find a better ride.

Unlike our first trip north, when we drove through the night, it was a bright sunny day.

The traffic was light, as I guided my not so spunky DeSoto around the same twisting highway.

My ride, while semi dependable, had to be pushed hard to come anywhere close to the speed of Paul's powerful big bore super charged Chrysler.

The first few, *slow to 25 mph,* corner re-enactments, went off without a hitch, although the DeSoto could barely surpass the posted speed limit.

This time of day, the only station I could find on the radio, no Wolfman Jack from Del Rio Texas, was KFAM, in Coeur d'Alene, Idaho.

The station had too much local talk for me, but it was now playing hit songs for their lunch crowd.

I turned up the radio volume, as I drove by the Good Reverend's farmhouse. I was just two miles from 'THAT DAMN CORNER,' as Paul referred to it.

I thought of it differently, more of a test of my manhood.

The highway was going down a gradual incline as the curve came closer. I had the Desoto fly around the sweeping turn before the sharp corner ahead. I glanced at the speedometer...Forty-Five mph.

I pushed down on the accelerator, the carburetor coughed. I zoned in on the *YELLOW SLOW TO 25mph* sign, stuck out my chin, and choked all the moisture out of the steering wheel.

Peter, Paul and Mary where singing *'Puff the Magic Dragon,'* on the radio.

And Puff I did. The only thing different, this time, was the car wasn't traveling fast enough to go airborne.

My slug of a car skidded through the loose gravel road shoulder, started to roll, but its forward momentum was insufficient to break the iron sled loose from mother earth.

I coughed from the dust rolling into my open vehicle. The motor spurted and died.

"Dumb shit," I said, before laughing at my predicament. "This corner sure as hell doesn't like me much."

All four of the car fenders, wrinkled from crashing through knee high broken rock, and drift wood debris.

Bottom line... the underpowered De Soto had saved me from myself. I started up my chariot and headed north to the Coeur d'Alene boat races.

Later I learned that without someone you knew to share the boat races with was not much fun. It was hard to raise hell when the people around you didn't see the humor in your antics.

*   *   *

39

A BRIDGE NOT TOO FAR

What's in a name? I had learned firsthand that in the Pacific Northwest, the colloquially know 'Chicken Hawk' is actually far from it.

The bird hardly ever targeted full sized chickens. The Red-tailed Hawk is a master of scanning for prey activity, from an elevated perch. It is deadly, once it has locked on to his victim below.

The Red-tailed Hawk's brick-red tail, with buff-orange feathers underside, pressed back against the steel railing, as it leaned downward scanning the water below.

His whitish underbelly feathers bristled in the slight breeze, like tiny fingers tickling piano keys.

Mister Hawk ignored at least one hundred humans picnicking and playing, on the waterfront of Heyburn State Park, just two hundred yards away.

The bird of prey sat on his favorite perch, the abandoned Chatcolet Railroad 3, one- hundred-foot long swing bridge.

The bridge, built in 1921, served the silver miles, discovered in the valley, in 1884. Its wingspan closed now, waiting for what future man had in store.

* * *

"*Kree-eee-ar*," pierced the air, the sound was a three second hoarse, rasping scream.

The once high-pitched noise slurred down to nothing.

"Was that a trail's steam whistle on the old tracks," asked the teenage boy, sitting on the beach, next to where I had spread out my beach towel.

I looked across the lake at the old railroad bridge. "Nah... just Mr. Hawk calling to his buddies," I said to the kid.

The hawk dropped off the bridge, following the railroad tracks, where they connected to the land, and landed on its prey.

"Looks like a rodent met his master," I said.

"So you were telling me about diving off those cliffs in Deep Lake... was it as high as where that hawk was sitting?"

"That's nothing... I've dove off one hundred and twenty feet before."

"Bullshit! Why not just jump instead dive?"

"Great rush... nothing like hitting the water face first, at breakneck speed," I said, standing up, looking at the two young high school girls I had been flirting with earlier.

"Lets go see if we can borrow their floats. We can paddle over to the bridge, and I'll show you who the bullshitter is."

Twenty minutes later, we floated up to the base of the railroad bridge. "You sure can sling the bull... can't believe they let us borrow their floats." The pimple faced boy said.

"You haven't seen anything yet cowboy,"

I said, feeling my oats.

I'll show this punk what a real man can do!

My second dive was from the control building's roof... I straddled the ridge and plunged 110 feet or more to the surface of Lake Couer D'Alenes.

*

HISTORIC CHATCOLET BRIDGE

I did a swan dive like the ones the Acapulco divers do off the cliffs, into the Sea of Cortez, Mexico. No sharks to worry about except for some boozed up onlookers.

ME DOING A DIFFERENT CRAZY HIGH DIVE

* * *

40

A PLUNGE TOO HIGH… DO IT TWICE AND REALLY LIVE

I swam, splashing my way to the right side of the swinging side of the bridge. After climbing on the rocks at the base of the span, I pulled my raft out of the water.

The bridge had a metal ladder rising out from the water level, extending to the top of the steel super structure.

"Hey kid… make sure my raft doesn't float away."

"How high is this thing?"

"Don't know for sure. I'll count the rungs going up."

I started up the ladder, counting the metal rungs, as I ascended, one at a time.

"Ninety-eight… ninety-nine… I'll be damn… one hundred exactly." I said, looking down at the kid.

"Wow! They look about a foot apart. Got to be a hundred feet." The kid said.

"You got it." I said. "I'm going to make my way to the middle."

A little winded from the climb, I stepped off onto the roof, next to a small building, of what looked like some kind of control or maintenance building for the bridge. There was another short metal ladder on its side.

I scooted up the ladder, walked out onto the roof, and looked down.

The kid, gawking at me from below, shielded his eyes

from the sun and said, "Wow, another ten feet or so."

The day was perfect... too perfect for a high dive.

A little breeze to break up the surface tension, on the water would be a lot safer.

But I had never met Mr. Safer. Not giving it another thought, I bent my knees, straightened, and pushed off the rooftop.

Just like all the pictures, I had seen about the Mexicans diving off the cliff in Acapulco, I arched my back and made a sweet swan dive into Lake Chatcolet.

I came to the surface to the roar of the kid and three people, in a small speedboat, idling next to the kids raft.

"What a bitchen dive buddy. Can I go get my camera, and will you do it again?" The guy, driving the boat asked.

I hung on the side with the kid's raft, looking at the guy, in the boat, with not one, but two hot looking women.

"Yeah sure," I said, not thinking it through, my male hormones raging.

*   *   *

Ten minutes later found me back at the top of the small building.

I looked out across the lake at the small armada of boats, headed my way. It was funny how everybody wanted to see a car wreck up close. That included me of course.

The first guy had spotted me climbing the ladder, and had driven over to check me out.

Getting a glimpse of my dive was a bonus for him, to show off for his girlfriends on board.

"Hey buddy we're ready... are you?" Yelled the first guy,

from his boat, surrounded by a half dozen others.

I gave them a small wave, and then stared down at the water. Something was a little different.

The water's surface was choppy now, from all the boat activity. This, I would recount later, saved me from some real muscle damage.

I blew my second attempt, part from fatigue, part from too much adrenalin. My hands not together, I over arched my back, hitting the water with a loud thud.

Nevertheless, from a dive from hundred and ten feet... the choppy water saved my bacon. My lucky break...if the water had been smooth, the surface tension could have broken many bones and organs.

Now, with a somewhat dislocated shoulder, if only I could reach the surface. I managed to surface next to the first guy's boat, and hand pulled my good arm towards safety.

I had become a folk hero of sorts, retelling my two dives repeatedly for the next hour, on the beach at Heyburn State Park. With each telling the dive became higher... more daring.

Two hours later, my shoulder somewhat reset, I spent the late afternoon, frolicking in the shallows with the boaters. Later, crashing alone in my car to recharge my batteries, I gave thanks that all my parts where still intact.

The ecstasy of my triumph gave way to my body's need to mend in peace.

* * *

41

JUST A SHORT FALL INTO A ROCK CRUSHER

My first job, after graduating high school, at S&S Sand and Gravel, Grant County, Washington, was almost my last job ever. Another risky job, and another (high-dive), only a few feet, could have been my final downfall.

While working on a rock crusher, in Eastern Washington, I had a job as the feeder operator.

My task was to stand on the metal catwalk running above the conveyor belt, feeding football-sized rocks into the nasty machine called Jaws, which took the first big bites out of rocks, fed into the rock crusher.

I held a red and green button control strip in my hand, to stop and let the rocks catch up. At my feet, lay a sledgehammer I used to break up any oversized rocks.

The constant noise of smashing granite rocks made it hard to hear any other sound at all. I worked most days a ten to twelve hour shift, six days a week. We worked in our assigned areas. I had not seen anybody for a few hours.

It was midday. The drone of machinery, and crushing rocks filled the hot dusty place, when I slipped on a sledgehammer, lying on the catwalk, in front of me, falling onto the conveyor belt, running to the jaws of death.

I tried to scramble out, but the conveyor ran too fast. My yells went unheard, over the maddening racket, going on below me.

As luck would have it, my foreman returned to check on me, a hunch he had *'about the boy,'* just in time to turn off the ten-ton crushing machine.

I was two seconds away from becoming ¾ inch minus, small enough pieces to fit through a ¾" by ¾" square holes, in a metal screen. Jaw's job was to gobble up the rocks, fed into it from the conveyor, and crush them into the consistency of course gravel.

A couple months back, a young worker, cleaning out the cone, where the loose rocks fall into the rock crusher, fell inside the mechanism while it was running.

His fate, what I barely escaped. His body came out of the piece of equipment as only blood, not any bones, or skin.

My destiny could have been to have the remnants of my body, spread out as a roadway, or walking path, and be driven over by vehicles, or tromped under foot by people, on their merry way to somewhere.

I went back to work the next day, no big deal!

*   *   *

42

A 120 MPH END-OVER-END... ALMOST MY END!

I was at my wits end so to speak. My dad was on my case. Possibly, WSU expelling me after my sophomore year, played a small part.

For sure he had over reacted... all I did was flunk out, and the little matter of a few ill-timed pranks. The older generation just didn't get it. There was plenty of time later on to study and act all grown up.

The summer of 1963, was hotter than usual, and I needed to reconnect with some of my fun high school buddies.

Most of the fellows my age had real a real job, and some with families already. I was kind of the class jester in high school. Many of the underclassmen thought I was *way cool*.

My pal Doug had a new paint job on his '58 Chevy Impala, and wanted to show it off to three other school chums and me. I sat in the back seat of the Impala with Ed Burns, while Doug drove, and John Bennar sat shotgun.

My posse, (*Hanger-oners*... The dictionary says 'A person who spends time in the company of another person, or of a group out of admiration, or for personal gain,') were all two years my junior, and a little star struck, because 'Rick was back in Ephrata.'

After only a dozen minutes of catching-up with volumes of BS, I slipped out of Doug's ride, and into the back door of the Sweet Grass Tavern.

Ten minutes later, I came back out of the beer joint, with a rack of beer under one arm. Doug opened the Impala's trunk, the customary high-five at the ready.

Just then, the local city police officer drove by, rounded the corner, and slowed down.

"Damn!" Doug said, while turning away to get back into the driver's seat.

"Let's roll," I said sliding into the back seat.

Doug drove away, careful not to speed. We all looked out the back window at the police car turning around. For sure, the long arm of the law decided to follow a car full of underage drinkers.

"Run for the edge of town. He'll never leave the city limits." I said, full of myself.

The police car's flashing lights came on. Doug, confidant in their local celebrity's assessment of the situation, pushed the Chevy to a hundred miles an hour.

We crossed the city limit sign as I tossed out the bottle of Gator Aid I had been nursing. Splat! The bottle smashed its contents on the police car's windshield. "Not good, Ed laughed."

"Doug, turn off your lights," I yelled. "Get to the Soap Lake road, and turn with your lights off."

With just barely enough moonlight to see the intersection, Doug turned and slowed down, stopping a hundred feet later, on the darker side of the roadway.

We looked out the rear, as the police car flew by the intersection behind. Doug, now full of himself, turned his headlights back on too soon. The police car's lights spun around in the distance, signaling Doug's big mistake.

Doug floored the Impala, fear of capture chiseled into his sweating face. Before we knew it, we were doing one hundred and twenty. With our windows down, the rushing air caused all our eyes to water. The small block Chevy revved to the breaking point, its commander strangling the vibrating steering wheel.

The roadway made a small turn to the right... but Doug miscalculated, making a slighter turn. The car's front tire dropped into the loose gravel. As if we were skating across a frozen lake, the Impala started to fish tail down the highway. Handing Ed my open bag of peanuts, I said, "Here have some... may be your last."

Later, the police officer enlightened my dad, "I counted at least seven end over end flips."

Somehow, we landed on all four wheels. And somehow I was alive. Not knowing for sure how I got out of the car, or how I came to my feet... I became a 'NON-Hanger-oner,' fleeing into the dark, for parts unknown.

* * *

LATER, EARLY IN THE MORNING... I STOOD IN THE EMERGENCY ROOM. Common sense had me check in on my old friends.

My return to small town stardom, resulted in Doug being thrown from his crashing car, with a broken shoulder and nose. John broke an ankle. Lucky for Ed and me, we just had some cuts and bruises.

My dad walked in, not happy. The police officer filled him in on our escape from reality, to crazy young men hell.

I had never heard him swear before, but he just unloaded on me. "*&%$##."

Dad pulled a pack of cigarettes out from my shirt pocket. He threw the cigs onto the floor. Then he jumped up and down on them, with his shinny Washington State Trooper boots, twisting the tobacco into the linoleum floor.   Dad felt, his son should never par take of the devil's wicked weed.

Dad and I drove back to the Sweet Grass Tavern, "Is this the gal that sold you the beer?" He asked. The red-faced woman had been selling me beer, out the back door, since I was nineteen.

The State of Washington removed the tavern's liquor license for a week. Country justice, I guess.

On our way back home, I knew my fate, and decided to beat my dad to the punch. "You don't have to worry about me anymore... I'm moving out." I said. After I packed a few things into a sad sack of a duffle bag, I walked out of my dad's house for good.

* * *

A couple of my early rides:

1950 Plymouth in 1963

1962 Pontiac

*   *   *

43

THE EARLY BIRD CAUGHT A RIDE

Three o'clock in the morning found me hitch hiking. A car pulled over, and a chap my age, never meeting before, asked me... "Where ya going fella?"

"California," I said.

"What's in California?"

"My buddy Ernie moved there. He said there's lots of work out in La La land."

"You can't get there tonight. You look like an ok guy. Want to spend the night at my place?"

Out of any real options, I accepted his kind offer.

It's funny how things can work out sometimes.

I became the fourth person in line of homeless guy's, who shared this young man's rental house. Cooler heads had prevailed that morning, being my hot head came around. Following Ernie, unprepared, to California, would have been a pipe dream full of pitfalls.

Having put aside some money, from my latest summer job, I bought a 1957 Chevy for two hundred and fifty dollars.

Now there was plenty of time to rethink the California dreamin' adventure, and not let it become another Ricky misadventure.

*   *   *

44

ONE GOOD ROLL DESERVES ANOTHER

I had been running my mouth about how cool the Omak Stampede Suicide Race was, to my roomies.

I told the guys who hadn't seen it before, "It's the deadliest horse race in the world. And it's in our backyard... right here in Washington!"

I always wanted to give the race a go... but not with Rego. Too many horses broke a leg and had to be put down, after falling down Suicide Hill.

The race started on the flat top of the appropriately named *Suicide Hill*. The riders would charge down the steep hill, swim their horses across a river at the bottom, and run their panting steeds a quarter mile to the crowd, waiting in the rodeo grounds

The rules stated that riders must wear helmets and lifejackets. Kind of sissy-fied, I thought.

But they say "it's the ultimate demonstration of the rider's ability to become one with the horse." I could relate to that.

Nevertheless, young and single young men needed to check it out, with plenty of cute cowgirls to go around.

The day of the Omak Stampede, another pal of mine, Jim Franklin, volunteered to drive two of my roommates and me, if we used my '57 Chevy.

Heck yeah, the other two guys paid for the gas.

A win-win for me, I thought.

We drove by some nice looking gals, decked out in nifty looking cowgirl outfits, walking down a steep hill, where the overflow crowd of spectators had parked.

While Jim tried to parallel park my Chevy on the steep hill, he became distracted, checking out the flirting gals.

The Chevy, with four horny, young, preoccupied studs, slid off the hillside, rolling over three times, before resting on all four wheels, at the little canyon's bottom.

My Chevy paid the price for Jim's distraction. Later, I had to put down my iron horse, like one of the horses that broke a leg in the race, descending Suicide Hill.

The four of us, survived our version of the suicide race. Our prize... we were ride-less in Omak, and over one hundred miles from home. So far, being both young and foolish, had not worked out for me... but he that doesn't remember his mistakes, will soon repeat them!

Rick Grimstead, through years of misconduct, became the poster child for that affliction.

*   *   *

PART FOUR

TARZAN MEETS HIS JANE

45

MEETING KAY

My WOMAN:

Meeting and hooking up with Kay Robertson became my saving grace, from a path of being unsuccessful in life.

I first saw Kay walking down the street in Ephrata. I asked my buddy, "Who's that?"

From that moment forward, she had a spell on me. The wonder of what it would be like to show her funny things I would do or say. I had thought that it's a smooth move being the guy, in the crowd, that makes everybody laugh. After all, doesn't every young lady like her man to make her smile? At some point, with Kay's help, I figured out that I needed to add some substance to my slap-stick antics, or people would never take me seriously.

I had been dating another senior girl in Coulee City, for about a year. My semi-girlfriend Claudia reamed me good, for not telling her about Kay. Not unusual for me, at the time. I was a free spirit, always on the lookout for a pretty lady to meet.

On the 4th of July that year, Kay and I had our first date. Like in the book about Tarzan (which means white skinned in ape language) Jane didn't exactly meet Tarzan. He kidnapped, her and carried her off, into the trees.

I thought about how a white skinned cowboy would rescue her from the big city of Ephrata, and carry her off to the sweet grasslands of Eastern Washington.

Unlike Tarzan's Jane, Kay had plenty of other options. So much for the Hollywood, one-sided love story, where the macho guy carries the day. But, this was the real world, with real issues, not made fun of, not for tomorrow.

* * *

46

OUT OF HAND GRENADE

"YOUR SON PULLED A PIN ON A HAND GRENADE, AND IS IN THE HOSPITAL," said the Washington State Trooper to Bob Grimstead. Dad and mom stood in the doorway of their motel room, in Burlington, Washington. Both were in total shock, but not in total disbelief.

After all, I always seemed to find the strangest ways to be in the news of the day. Mom and dad were in Western Washington visiting family, over two hundred miles from their dying son.

A hand grenade, are you kidding?

They all thought... *no one ever lives, after being that close to an exploding, body ripping hand grenade.*

Through the night Bob and Ada drove, with dread on their hearts. But alas... it was just another one of my many foo-paws.

Kay had moved out of her family house. Her new roommate, Sandy Wiley, had a date with a fellow named Tom, who was going to start the Naval Academy next term.

We were all leaving to go out for a dinner/dance.

After the girls left the room, I spotted a plastic green grenade sitting on the windowsill.

"What's this?" I asked Tom, holding up the grenade.

"I got it at the navy base last weekend. It's only a smoke bomb," Tom said with a proud look on his face.

"Wouldn't it be cool to fill the girl's room with smoke," I said. Imagining how nifty I would seem to the others.

"I don't think..."

I cut Tom off before he could finish, and pulled out the pin. "Nothing... must be a dud." I said.

Then a spoon shaped device popped out of the grenade, followed by a hissing sound. It smelled strong, like some kind of tear gas device... something bad.

I held the grenade at arms length, not so sure this would turn out cool anymore. "Let's get this thing out of here," I said, just as the grenade exploded.

The explosion filled the small room with not cool blue smoke. Instead, with shredded plastic bits, and eye burning, throat clogging tear gas.

Falling to the floor, blinded by the blast, my eyes pulsed with pain... that I had never felt before.

Mike Strathern, one of Kay's neighbors, pulled me out of her room, and into his bathroom. He flooded my eyes with water, from the faucet, but no relief came.

"Mike, are my eyes cut?" I asked.

"To shreds," Mike said, helping me sit down on his toilet.

* * *

THE DARK MADE STARS IN MY MIND

I lay on my hospital bed, listening to our dinner party guests, asking the doctor about my condition.

"Well son, this is what your mom and I drove through the night to see?" I heard my dad say, in the background.

I could make out my parents looking down at me. My vision had returned, but my eyes sore as heck, tears flooding down my cheeks. "Nice to see you mom," I said. She smiled back at me, shaking her head a little.

Dad had enough of his not so special offspring, and walked out of the room. In a week's time, I had recovered, and put this little setback behind me.

Tear Gas Burns Eyes In Basin

EPHRATA — Six young people, about to leave for a dance here Saturday night, found out about tear gas when one of them pulled the pin on a plastic tear gas grenade, thinking it was not real.

Rich Grimstead, 21, was hospitalized for observation when the gas exploded into his face. He had recovered and was back at work today.

Mike Strathern, who went to his aid, was treated at Columbia Basin Hospital and released.

The apartment of Kay Robertson and Sandy Wiley was still too full of tear gas to be used Sunday night, according to an Ephrata police department report. Tom Nelson and Leslie Pendleton also suffered from burning eyes.

A friend had left the grenade in the apartment earlier, without explanation.

Above is a newspaper clipping I added to my scrapbook of misdeeds. Not exactly the same kind of clipping my dad had accumulated, through his top-notch sports career.

A proud pop he was not!

*   *   *

47

TWO LOVES OF MY LIFE COME TOGETHER

During my first year at WSU, my dad needed to free himself from taking care of Rego. He put him out to pasture in Soap Lake, Eastern Washington.

Two years later, after my sophomore year, and when I started dating Kay, I took her to see Rego, and go for a ride.

He remembered our times together, and was chomping at the bit, after I slipped it into his mouth, ready to go. I wanted to impress my new gal with my riding skills.

Shortly after mounting up, I had him at a full gallop. Kay sat behind me... hanging onto my waist with a death grip. She had never been on a horse before that day.

I told everybody that asked how Kay liked riding Rego... "She really enjoyed it!"

Truth be known... she was scared shitless, but did not let on. Like when someone is driving like crazy down a twisting mountain road, feeling oneness with your maker, while your passenger is hanging on, by grasping anything solid, with their fingernails.

Why is it that some people's joys are other people's nightmares? ... Go figure.

* * *

48

OUR WEDDING DAY

December 30, 1964 was a snowy day in Ephrata, Washington. It was below zero degrees outside, but the warm of hearts of family, gathered inside the Methodist Church.

Because of the bad weather, many of our friends and family, from Western Washington, were unable to attend.

However, it was our wedding day. Kay and I were determined to tie the knot, come hell or high snowdrifts.

Gerry K. Robertson Becomes Bride Of Richard Grimstead

The wedding reception ended about 9:00 PM, because of the bad weather, and our guests needed to get home safe.

Of course, I feared no man or a little snow blizzard, so off Kay and I went to our honeymoon, in Sand Point, Idaho. It was every new bride's dream honeymoon... a below zero snow, ski adventure, in white out conditions.

Three AM found us pulling Kay's sleek 1954... not really, white Oldsmobile, into our honeymoon's motel parking lot.

I did not put snow tires on her car for two reasons; first real men don't need *any stupid safety equipment,* and money was in short supply.

It was bright, and early, 7:00 AM, and we were late heading out to the Swisher Basin Ski Resort, for our first day of skiing. Also was too late for a morning of marital bliss.

There was one small problem... Kay had never skied before.

Adding to my manly dilemma... was a ton of fresh snow powder, waiting for my attention on the upper slopes.

So, like any newly married man, I made sure I gave Kay, a few minutes of my precious time, instructing her on the art of snow plowing, on the bunny hill.

I checked on her after a few dozen runs, and found she was snowplowing quite well... at least in my eyes.

On the second morning, being the expert I am, in assessing other people's skill levels... I decided it was time to move her up from the lame rope tow, to riding the chair lift.

Like the gentleman I am, I helped her scoot onto the chairlift. As we approached the top of the chairlift, I sensed some tension in her demeanor, and gave her more advice.

"Kay... it's a piece of wedding cake. Just stand up, keep your knees bent slightly, take a deep breath, and let your momentum carry the day."

BAM!

Kay ran into me, and we both fell into a bundle of legs, ski poles and twisted bodies. I bought her a cheap pair of wooden skis, to save money, and both of the ski's tips now busted.

After stepping out of her skis, I had her stand behind me, as a passenger would do, on a motorcycle. My plan was to ski us both down the run to the lodge. After several failed attempts to pull this off, she gave up, and walked down the ski slope, to the lodge below.

Kay was not a happy camper.

I scraped enough money together, and rented her some good equipment. For the next three days, she became proficient at mastering the art of beginning Alpine skiing.

I was a proud hubby.

We were both on an up note... but now it was time to return Ephrata to start our new life together, as newlyweds.

The people in the lodge told us a big storm was coming. We had better get on the road and try to beat the storm, or the roads may not be open.

When we got to Spokane, there was a cold gentle rain falling. I thought, perhaps we left too soon, and could have skied a couple more days. Boy was I wrong!

As we ascended Sunset hill, leaving Spokane, we hit the leading edge of the promised storm. The blinding snow made it almost impossible to see ahead. I saw what looked like a yellow caution light, telling me to slow down. I found out later, it was actually a flashing light, above a road closed, sign. *'Damn the Torpedoes Full Speed Ahead,'* was said by, Rear Admiral David G Farragut, of the US Navy. His words came to mind, spoken during the Battle of Mobile, in the American Civil War.

This was my battle. I had to get my bride safely back to Ephrata, in one piece. This was my kind of challenge.

The snow drifts started out just bumper high, as I hit them, going seventy miles an hour. The drifts slowed us down a little, then I would accelerate back to seventy, until hitting the next one.

I hit hood high the next snow drift, slowing down to almost nothing. A half mile later, after returning to seventy, I hit the mother lode of snowdrifts.

Boom White Chocolata! It was as high as our roof.

The forward momentum, of the two-ton car, came to almost a dead stop, before surging forward again.

We limped into a gas station, in Davenport, Washington. A while later, exhausted from our ordeal, an attendant walked up and said, "First car in hours. You must be doing something important."

"On our way home, from our honeymoon," I said, leaning out the car window.

"Only seen police, ambulances, and a crazy or two," the attendant said.

"How is the road to Ephrata?" I asked.

"Lots of drifts, but nothing like the road to Spokane... been closed for two days. Snow plows can't even get through."

"That's the way we came, just now."

"Impossible. The State Patrol said some drifts are twenty feet high."

"I guess that would make us the third crazy you've seen today... because we sure did come from that direction."

The attendant finished filling our gas tank, shaking his head, probably not believing me.

This would be a honeymoon to remember for sure! Unparalleled by some of our friends honeymoon to lush tropical locations, funny colored adult beverages, with little straw umbrellas, stuff of boredom, I am sure.

*　*　*

49

THE MISSLIE SILO DISMANTLING PROJECT...

was located near Moses Lake, Washington, summer of 1966.

The best paying summer job I ever had, and for good reason. Because the extreme danger involved, in the demolition work, resulted in at least two other WSU summer helpers being killed while working on the Eastern Washington State project.

Some other fatalities, and serious injuries, occurred in several neighboring states, with The Minuteman Missile Sites and their connected support facilities.

During the Cold War, congress allocated many millions of taxpayer dollars to dig deep holes in the ground, in remote areas. This was our way of concealing our deadly intercontinental nukes underground, and out of sight of the Ruskies.

The Titan Missile Silos averaged over one-hundred and twenty-foot deep, with steel reinforced concrete walls. Inside the concrete tubes, was a substructure of catwalks, to access electrical, plumbing, and ventilation systems.

When the Cold War ended, congress allocated millions of U.S. taxpayer dollars, to remove the hardware, from the now empty silos.

Most WSU students had safe summer jobs in supermarkets, gas stations and such.

I liked the riskier jobs, because that's where the real money for the taking, was offered to the brave young souls.

I ignored the job's safety orders, falling head first, down a hundred and twenty-foot deep Titian Missile Silo. The job related accident was NOT my fault, not a hundred percent my fault.

At an early age, I learned to respect the military style authority. My state trooper father, instructed me to obey superiors, and follow their rules. No matter how dumb, stupid, or difficult they seemed to me.

I learned to comply with my elders and teachers, or suffer the consequences of my actions. However, I still had a lot of common sense to learn, at just barely twenty.

* * *

My duties were to uninstall the various types of hardware, fastened to the walls of the silo, for salvage. *Haste makes waste*, not in my vocabulary. A *task done the quickest, was the best choice.*

First safety rule; always tell someone what you are working on. Second safety rule; always tie off to the silo structure, when not working on the open elevator. Third safety rule, the elevator was our working platform, never work under it without telling someone.

Lucky me, I won the Tri-fecta, breaking all three rules the same day. As in wagering at a horse racing track. Only lucky for me, my payoff was never realized. I got to live and fight another day.

I was unfastening hardware, from the silo wall, just below the elevator platform, at the top of the silo shaft.

Sweaty palms, poor lighting, and unstable footing, on a hot dusty day, in any order, was an accident waiting to happen. And it did!

I lost my footing, and fell head first, down the one-hundred and twenty-foot shaft.

An angel, lucky ducky, or good timing, wrapped a large wrench, hanging from my belt, on a rope, around a steel crossbeam, broke my fall. I swayed backed a forth, then reached out, and pulled on the twelve-foot rope, grabbing a hold of the steel frame.

I looked up, and saw that I had fallen to a depth of about twenty feet, from the bottom of the elevator platform. Taking in a deep breath, I closed my eyes, thanking whomever for saving my life.

BZZZZZ went the motor on the elevator platform. It was coming down. I either would be crushed, or knocked off my perch, to my sudden death.

"Hey! Hey! Hey!" I screamed with all my voice.

I was dancing around trying to free myself, from the silo's sideway, knowing I was going to die anyway.

Bang! Bang!

The two-foot long pipe wrench clanged, hitting the metal elevator shaft framework. It was hanging from the rope, around my waist, but caught onto the steel structure, just over my head.

The elevator suddenly stopped, inches, from crushing me to into a bloody slime on the silo's steel framed walls.

"Hey! Hey!" I yelled out.

"Is that you Rick," asked my foreman, leaning over the edge of the platform, eye balling dumb shit me. "Only heard the clanging of the wrench... didn't hear you until now.

Count your lucky stars... should be dead son."

You'd think that would've been the end of my time at the silo. The contractor needed help still. I just sluffed it off, as a little bad luck. However, I knew better to play by the rules from now on, at least on this job.

* * *

A typical one-hundred and twenty-foot-deep Titan Missile Silo, with the BAD GUY ready to launch, at the former USSR, if needed.

We removed all of the non-nuclear support hardware in the shaft. This work was started, right after the Titan Missile was relocated to a secret location during the night.

50

ROBIN EGG BLUE SURPRISE

In the summer of 1967, after our first son Darren was born, Kay and I were living in a dollar a night motel.

I was a new college grad now, but the only work I could find was for a local farmer, at a dollar twenty-five an hour, on his sprinkler moving gang.

We were down to our last fifty bucks, with not much on the horizon, to decrease our financial woes.

A ten-hour dusty day, in the farming fields behind me, I steered Kay's old white '54 Oldsmobile sedan down the gravel road, fronting the irrigation water canal.

In a daydream, about our future, I did not realize the gravel road made a gradual right turn.

SNAP!

I turned the steering wheel to the right, but the car continued going straight off the road.

Before I knew it, the car slipped off the canal's rocky edge, plunging into the running water.

Somewhere between the car hitting the water, and settling on the canal's bottom, I was able to swim to the surface, and climb out onto the bank.

I sat on the bank staring at the oil slick on the swirling water. *Lucky break... I had not drowned,* I thought.

Then reality sunk in. *What now... what will Kay think?*

The only good news... it was a short walk to Bob's auto wrecking business.

Bob was sympatric to my problem, and listened, as I explained about being broke, with a young wife.

"Let's get your car out of the water first. Then I may have a deal for you," Bob said to me.

* * *

Twenty minutes later, I was thirty-feet down at the bottom of the canal, wrapping a chain around the Old's front bumper.

Back at the wrecking yard Kay's white Olds sat in the yard, as Bob and one of his guys checked it out.

"You broke a tie rod. Lucky for you, it didn't happen on a busy street." Bob said.

"Yeah lucky I am," I said, lighting up a smoke.

"How 'bout the deal of the century Rick? Follow me out back," Bob said, walking ahead, without waiting. I stood next to where Bob had stopped walking, starring in awe, at a '59 Olds hard top convertible, painted Robin Egg Blue.

A real thing of beauty to a down and out loser. I thought, wanting to pinch myself to make sure this was happening.

"The owner blew up both the engine and tranny." Bob said, waiting for me to say something.

"Wish I could afford..."

Bob interrupted me, "Can you come up with fifty?"

"Are you joking?"

"I said, deal of the century."

The next day, I drove away my Robin Egg Blue Oldsmobile, out of Bob's wrecking yard. He had swapped out the engine and tranny, from Kay's old beater.

In my mind it was a beater, Kay thought otherwise. It had served her well at WSU.

She loved our new wheels, and the lucky break Bob had given us.

*   *   *

PART FIVE

FROM THE HILLS OF MONTAZUMA

JARHEAD TIME

51

USMC DEBACLES

While in college, in 1965, I received a notice to take the physical exam for the army. Thinking because I was married, and a college student, I would not be DRAFTED.

Because I had screwed-up (flunked out), I was to report to the Army, as Private Richard Grimstead.

I applied for reinstatement with the ROTC at WSU. Even though I had two years of being in the ROTC, before dropping out, they would not take me back. Also, because of flunking out in college.

I asked the Airforce, after checking with the Army, and they said no as well.

Last, I tried the Marine Corp, because I wanted to be a commissioned officer, and not a grunt enlisted man.

I was starting my junior year at WSU. The recruiter asked me what I wanted to do? I really didn't know. He asked me if I would like to go to flight school.

I said, "Yeah... like be a pilot?"

A light went on in my brain... I would get to go real fast... do fun and crazy things?

The recruiter said I needed to take a few tests, to see if I had the RIGHT STUFF!

I took the tests, and got a call a little later, from the recruiter saying, "Rick... you passed the tests. Congrats... you are in the program."

To avoid the draft, and joining the ground forces in Viet Nam, I signed up with the Marine Corp, and became a commissioned officer.

For the next two years, I kept getting letters from the commandant of the Marine Corps, at the OCS (Officer's Candidate School), saying how he was looking forward to meeting me.

I was thinking maybe he wanted to hang out with me... play squash... have a beer?

WRONG!

I had seen movies about Westpoint, and the Naval Academy, and figuried that I was going to be doing something similar.

Wrong again!

Not so fast easy going country boy! Any daydreams of an easy term, were put to rest, when I discovered how tough base camp was, on an out of shape slacker. I did some research, and found out some things they would expect me to complete, in my training.

Requirements included; running three miles under thirty minutes, a certain number of pushups, pull-ups, sit-ups, and squats.

With six months left before my reporting for duty, I tried some of the exercises. I did kinda okay, running the three miles, in just under the required thirty minutes.

No big deal, I can do this, I thought.

52

IT'S THE REAL DEAL RICKY BOY!

It isn't for the faint of heart, or party boy slacker.

I arrived at Officers Candidate School at Quantico, Virginia... in the summer of 1967.

Right out of the chute... I got a standard military hairdo... a shaved dome. The first sign that I did NOT control my own body anymore.

I had barely any time to admire my new look, when they plowed us into the physical tests. The same tests that I had pooh-poohed, as going to be a piece of cake for me.

First, the required ten pull-ups.

The drill sergeant made me stop halfway down, on number ten and hold my position.

My arms were on fire, as I struggled to stay firm, and not go to the bottom. He said, "okay, turn your hands around... let yourself come to a dead hang at the bottom." I hung with my arms burning, my feet a foot from the floor.

"Give me one more candidate!" The drill instructor yelled at me.

I was spent! I had nothing left in the tank.

"Drop out Pussy. Give me forty push-ups!" The drill sergeant said.

I did the forty pushups; I always had done. The sergeant said, "Not like that! Touch your chest to the floor, on each one."

I had never done pushups like that before, and could only do three more.

My three-mile run was just barely under the thirty-minute maximum, falling short on all the other required minimums also.

We had a Company of two hundred candidates, in various shapes and sizes.

They had us all gather around the drill sergeants for our results.

"Candidate Roberts, come forward." The head sergeant barked out.

A five-foot eight-inch tall, one hundred and thirty-five-pound young man, took the stage.

"Candidate Roberts scored a perfect one hundred on all the tests. Every Candidate looked impressed.

"Candidate Grimstead come forward," The drill sergeant said.

I looked around, unsure why they wanted me. I climbed onto the stage, as directed.

"We have a new low," said the Company Captain, who had moved forward, to address the men. "This candidate scored the lowest, on every single test."

Things were off to a rocky start.

I am... the biggest shit-bag of all the two hundred men...

* * *

53

WANNA-BE NINJA WARRIOR

I had come to OCS two hundred and thirty pounds of bad eating habits, struggling big time, on many forced runs and hikes. My locker stuffed full of demerits.

The hikes were actually runs with fifty-pound packs and rifles... not easy for fat guys.

Most candidates could do the three-mile run in eighteen to twenty minutes. I caught the flu at the end of three weeks, the same time of our first big hike, which slowed me down and broke my confidence.

After seven weeks of training, all the recruits stood before the 'Speedy Board,' a group of officers that evaluated them and culled out the hopeless cases.

I told Kay that I would not still be here after the 'Speedy Board.' The only reason I was still in OCS was Vietnam.

Many front line Marines were being killed. It was simply a numbers game.

Sixty pounds lighter after eleven weeks, made running a lot easier. The drill captain would single me out half way through the run, making me do calisthenics. He would hold my feet together during sit-ups.

I asked him, "Do you think you can keep up with me now?" He laughed at me, and I said, "I'll do ten more than you in two minutes."

He agreed. We did, I beat him by ten more sit-ups. Over time, things where coming easier for me.

The big deal was when we came to the 'American Gladiator Drills.'

The captain singled me out when we started using the *Pugil Sticks,* (A heavy padded pole-like training weapon used since the 1940s to train military personnel for bayonet and rifle training.)

I was still his favorite dummy to pick on, and he did. He showed the candidate s how to use the horizontal and vertical strokes.

He beat the crap out of me.

At the end of the drills, after I had figured it out, I asked him, "Does the candidate ever get to go one on one, with the captain?"

"You wanta go at me?" The captain smirked at me.

"Yeah... I do!"

The first rattle out of the box, (an old cowboy expression meaning... prompt action or in the UK it means... straight way!) I knocked him down to the canvas.

We did it two more times, all with the same embarrassing results for him. I was much lighter on my feet and too quick for him now. I used to do a lot of street fighting as a kid. Now that I had my strength back, things came easy again.

I had paid my dues, no longer the laughing stock of the outfit. I had finally become a force to be reckoned with, not provoked anymore.

* * *

54

FLIGHT SCHOOL ANTICS

My time in flight school was eighteen months, from January, 1968 to June, 1969 in Pensacola, Florida.

Pilot training requirements shifted upward, at the Naval Air Station, Pensacola Florida, to meet the demands for the Vietnam War.

I lived off base with Kay and our son, in a single wide mobile home.

It was a postcard perfect morning. The cobalt blue sky, with a line of cotton candy shaped cumulus clouds, daring an adventurous chap, to make a flying run, around them.

I had already completed the maneuvers in my T28 trainer that I needed to perform.

T-28s at flight school

Not to mention, a 300 mph back roll that topped 10 G's, just for kicks.

Something a little more challenging... aka more fun ran through my mind. One of the clouds resembled a white Pillsbury Dough Boy version, of the Liberty Bell.

A message rang out to me, as if coming from that bell cloud, dead ahead. I always loved to slalom snow ski downhill, around evergreen trees, at break neck speed.

That image flashed in my mind.

Time to give 'er a go Rick! I thought.

Only spice it up a little oh-boy... would I!

So spice it up I did. Not just a simple level flight zig zag, around the clouds.

I steered the trainer over on its side, the plane's belly, almost rubbing the edge of each cloud, as I flew past.

While making a turn around the third cloud, a flash from something caught my eye. Directly overhead, not more than the length of my airplane away, another idiot was doing the same maneuver, in the opposite direction.

We survived a two hundred miles an hour head-on, near miss. Our planes roared past each other... belly to belly. I caught only a fleeting glimpse of my mirror image, in the other plane's cockpit.

I figured I was the only fool looking for that special feeling, which only comes with over the edge aerobatics.

Wonder if either one of us will get busted for this, I chuckled to myself.

* * *

Of course, I was a little gun shy, about getting into more air born trouble. Just a month earlier, while flying a night mission, I reached to crush my cigarette out in the dark cockpit, missing the astray.

The smoldering cig ended up in the night light console.

Then I had a brain fart... I put out the fire I had started, not with a fire extinguisher... with my half cup of coffee. This smooth move knocked out all my lights and instruments. I was now flying blind.

Making me fly home, on a wing and a prayer...

so to speak.

Thank goodness, it was a clear moonlit night, without overcast skies, because someone else would have been telling this story. The sad tale would be about a dumbass, showoff rookie pilot, crashing his out of fuel plane, into mother earth.

* * *

55

FLYING OUT OF CONTROL

Close to mother earth gyrations, proved to be, just as crazy as airborne flips and rolls.

I had a lot of time, out of the aircraft, on the ground and needed something to recharge my juices.

Not too far, back in time, I was a youngster, in need of a motorcycle, more like a craving for a Honda 250.

My dad had other ideas for his already spoiled son.

I was a grown man, married with a baby boy, finally getting that motorcycle. Actually, a little better... a 305 Honda scrambler.

Shortly afterward, I started entering enduros, an off-road motorcycle event, that focused on the endurance of the rider. My cup of tea... only it took awhile to get the hang of it, by not going fast as possible, all the time.

The part I liked the most... a variety of special tests, on different kinds of terrain. Especially the speed stages, where the fastest time, is what is happening.

* * *

On a warm afternoon, I was riding my 305, steering it around a favorite serpentine, asphalt country roadway.

Think of Lombard Street, in San Francisco, cork screwing its way, up to the clouds. Only as flat as a pancake, Florida roller-coaster, but with just as tight of turns, as Lombard Street.

I was going 30 mph, on a road where 15 mph was pushing it, just to stay on the pavement.

One goosed up twist of the bike's throttle too many, brought me facing head on, to a Ford station wagon, going at a snail's pace towards me.

I had to push myself up, and jump off the motorcycle. I landed with my palms knocking into the station wagon's windshield. The shattered mass of safety glass, landed into the lap of the driver. I rolled off the car, falling hard to the pavement, scraping my palms and knees on the asphalt.

Better to have dumb luck than no luck at all. The station wagon's driver was a flight surgeon, at the flight school. He was more concerned about my well-being, than the damage to his car.

After convincing the flight surgeon I was all right, I found my 305 scrambler.

It was still standing upright, in the woods, resting against a tree.

My ride home, a little reminder of what some people believe... *haste makes waste.*

The Honda's clutch lever was broken off. I had to drive the bike home power shifting, without a clutch, grinding the gears.

Still though... what a cool twisting ride I had made. Minus, a little repair work, the next day.

*   *   *

Kay pinning on my wings at the flight school graduation.

Below is my modest way of showing pure joy, in our back yard, later that day.

NAS Pensacola Pilot training, in 1969, produced 2,552 graduates. I became one of the fortunate sons.

Just like in the Creedence Clearwater Revival song, *'Fortunate So,.'* released that same year. I was indeed fortunate, not to be a foot soldier, tromping through the green hell of Vietnam.

Those were unfortunate SONS... with a gun... and little else. for my part, my young family below... top gun!

Careful what you ask for... I found out later.

Being high over the jungle, with only a shield of fragile plexiglass, gave the Viet Cong lots of pop shots at me, in my whirly bird flying duck.

After a year and a half of flight school, Kay, Darren, Eric and I went to El Toro Marines Base, in Tustin, California. In a couple of weeks, I was to start my tour, in Vietnam.

But first, I had to say goodbye to an old friend... if I could locate him.

*   *   *

56

REGO ONE LAST TIME

I had orders to go to Vietnam and didn't know if or when I was coming back to Eastern Washington.

And I had some loose ends to tie up.

Knowing my predicament, my dad stepped up and drove me around to find where Rego had landed.

It turned out Rego had five owners, since dad sold him all where along the Columbia River Valley.

Rego kept throwing off his new owners. None of them could make him stop.

Finally, we were face to face to owner number five, a Banker in Twisp, Eastern Washington.

"I understand you have a horse named Rego?" I asked.

"I do... It's my wife's. She loves that horse."

"Would the horse be about twelve or thirteen years old?"

"Oh no. This horse is only seven years old."

"Well, has it got one white foot and a blaze face?

"Yeah," the banker said, looking confused.

"Well, I broke that horse, and he is twelve or thirteen. Can we go see it? Can I ride him one last time?"

The banker smiled at us, and said, "Sure why not?"

* * *

Later that afternoon, we met up with the banker and his wife, at the Twisp Rodeo Grounds.

As luck would have it... the rodeo grounds had been set up for an equestrian event. Right up my wheelhouse, for captaining my ole friend.

They had poles set up for a pole bending course. Seeing this, I approached Rego... stared into his eyes, until I felt he remembered my face. He snorted a welcome and I mounted up on my old friend.

Just like hopping right back onto a bike after a fall... we became one again.

I slapped his flank, showing the gawking on-lookers, what a champion horse and rider could do together.

My second time through, the banker's wife timed my run. A very respectable twenty-four seconds.

The banker's wife had only been using Rego as a trail horse, but caught the bug, wanting to learn how to compete with Rego.

I worked with the banker's wife, showing her where Rego's control button was located.

Next, we worked on barrel racing with Rego, spinning and sliding on cue.

She became real efficient on Rego's back, winning a bunch of prizes and ribbons, over the following years.

I left for war, knowing my old buddy was reclaiming his youthful need to have some fun. He could relive the things that I had taught him to enjoy.

*   *   *

PART SIX

IN COUNTRY – (VIETNAM)

57

THE GREEN HELL - VIETNAM

The Marine Corps began aviation participation, in Vietnam, on Palm Sunday 1962, to save the world from the forces of evil.

I found it ironic, that Jesus Christ rode into Jerusalem on Palm Sunday, 0032, a mere nineteen-hundred and thirty years earlier, to save the world from other forces of evil also.

A squadron of UH-34 helicopters had landed at Soc Trang, in the Delta, with palm branches swaying in the wind, from the whirly birds.

Jesus rode bareback in on Donkey number 1, landing at the Jewish Holy Temple, with palm branches waiving overhead, at his feet, by the people who loved him.

The first squadron in Vietnam was Marine Medium Helicopter Squadron 362 (HMM-362.)

The squadron accompanying Jesus was the original group called (The 12), his disciples.

   *   *   *

My arrival in COUNTRY, was a lot less promising than the two aforementioned, not on Palm Sunday, Easter, Christmas, or even Ground Hog's Day.

It was the first week of November 1969, at 2 AM, in Denang airport, a mere week removed from Halloween, and all the goblins, ghouls and ghosts.

To add to a dismal start, thousands of mosquitoes descended on me, instead of Christian well-wishers.

The present Christian Messiah had come to fulfill his mission of salvation.

The former WSU slacker had come to Vietnam to fulfill his tour of country.

Welcome to your new home Rick! I hope and pray mine turns out better than being hung on a cross.

*   *   *

My first impressions after deplaning... it was unbelievably HOT and Humid; much more than even sticky Florida had been.

I spent that night, and the next day in a screened in porch, with the other greenhorns spread out in upper and lower bunks.

It was a night from hell... I never slept. *How can I make it for a year?* I thought. The fact was my first day was more than just awful.

The next day, I caught the first break I needed.

The Marine Corps assigned me to live in a Quonset hut, with four rooms, tile floor, air conditioning, very nice for the area. It had four men to a room. Luck of the draw, I guess.

Many of the newbies had to flop into little more than hard-walled tents, with only fans to cool them off, day or night.

My luck was getting even better. The big one! There were surfboards at a shack just down the beach, from our assigned sleeping area.

Above is a typical troop Vietnam style Hootch, with no AC, and lots of human sweat to pass around. The screened in porch I slept in the first night... was not any better.

*   *   *

58

THE EVERYDAY JARGON

The Vietnam Marine's, not so secret job talks.

There was a lot of jargon used in Nam. I picked up most of them fast.

Many of the terms were carryovers from both WW2, and the Korean War. Many derived from mixing with the local Vietnamese people.

Some of the jargon was spoken in front of anybody present, while others only shared between fellow Scuffys.

The piss-off of all jargons, was JODY... meaning the person who takes away you wife or girl, while you are stuck in Nam. We would use the song about Jody, in cadence, to do some drills.

It goes something like... "Ain't no use in goin' home... Jody's got your girl and gone... sound off...."

The number one favorite jargon was... GHOSTING meaning... goldbricking or sandbagging or f... ing off...

HUMP... meaning to march or hike, carrying a heavy rucksack, or to perform a balls breaking task.

NO SWEAT... not from the humidity, it meant and still to this day... can do... easy-peasy.

A new troop replacement was a CHERRY.

FRIENDLIES were U.S. troops, allies, or anyone not on the dark side.

Military maps were called COMIC BOOKS.

TALLY or TALLY-HO, I would say to my copilot when I spotted something, or a LZ, when I wanted him to see.

NUMBER ONE was the best thing.

NUMBER TEN... not so much... the worst. Although Bo Derrick had a good run at number ten.

A JOHN WAYNE was a can opener. Also, a loose cannon type of person, because of his actions of exposing himself to danger, with little regard of the consequences. Think of all the movies John Wayne made, blazing ahead, full speed, regardless of how it affected other people around him.

He put many people in danger, not a plus in Vietnam.

An interesting slant on how John Wayne was perceived in Vietnam read...

*Robert Flynn's essay, "John Wayne Must Die."

* * *

Also, there were some PG-13 to R rated Nam slang terms that are common in today's American slang.

Some are just as funny as their X rated cousins.

However, they are somewhat over-the-top... depending on one's point of view, or political persuasions.

JESUS NUT was the main rotor-retaining nut, that held the main rotor onto the rest of the helicopter.

The saying about it goes like this... 'If the Nut came off, only Jesus could help you.' Long odds... even for the Bible Thumpers.

HONEY-DIPPERS were the people responsible for burning human excrement.

BOOKOO was a French-ish, Vietnamese expression for "lots of..." anything.

GUNG HO... dare I say a John Wayne type. Balls to the wall... damn the torpedoes.

North Vietnamese regular soldiers were called GOMERS. Gomer Pile maybe?

The most used term to identify any people of Asian descent was... GOOKS. The Korean War vets used it in Korea as well.

KOON SA the wacky weed... Mary Jane.

DINKY DAU was Vietnamese for "You're crazy."

CYA a great tool on the internet... cover your ass.

PUCKER FACTOR was the original 'fear factor,' as how in the world can I pull this upcoming mission off?

The saying, 'When in Rome do as the Roman's do,' did not work with BA-MA-BA meaning "33" Vietnamese beer or, as we liked to call it, "Tiger Piss."

If you didn't get killed with a VC bullet... a horny Snuffy could pay a prostitute three to five dollars for a BOOM BOOM: "short time." VD could sometimes be a "short time" away, as well.

HOOTCH was our house or living quarters. Also, we used the term for "weed" or "booze."

K-BAR was not a Hershey candy bar. It was a Marine's favorite toy, also sometimes his salvation. A combat knife with a six-inch blade and hard leather handle.

LZ was for landing zone

MIKE-MIKE or MAD MINUTE meant to concentrate fire of all weapons for a short time, at maximum rate.

PIGS AND RICE or ASH AND TRASH: Non-combative mission flights, moving Marines to or from the field, to or from the rear base camp. And delivering hot food to the field or vacating men.

ASS AND TRASH meant moving people and their stuff to the field, not just some troops per say.

*　*　*

59

MY CHOCOLATE-COOKIE BAKING GRANDMA

Didn't follow me to Vietnam. But the F word sure did, in the X rated jargons.

Like the standup comedians doing jokes in a bar or a movie, there is something about vulgar terms that allows some people to let go of deep seated fears and laugh... if only for a moment.

Some of the terms, I heard Snuffy's (fellow Marines) used to mak task at hand bearable:

HAM N'MOTHERF...ers: C-Ration 'Ham and Lima Beans,' a well-hated meal among us all.

SNAFU: Situation Normal All F...ed Up

SHIT was our catch all phrase. If you were in a firefight you were in shit. Any bad situation was 'deep shit'.

And my favorite ('shit wired tight,') meant you were primed and ready for action.

DU was for the F-word. Like 'Whatever Dude' is in today's lingo.

And of course FUBAR meaning "F...ed Up Beyond All Recognition"

Oh how sweet it was... growing up in Vietnam!

*　*　*

"Vietnam was what we had instead of happy childhoods."
–Michael Herr, 1977

60

THIS IS FUBAR COUNTRY

... a Vietnam War acronym for...

"F...ed Up Beyond All Recognition"

I flew six hundred combat missions in Vietnam, and was awarded twenty-nine Air Medals.

On almost all of my helicopter recon missions, I was shot at, had many narrow escapes and some near death mishaps, by my own creation.

I jumped right into action, starting my first day. Sitting in the co-pilot seat, the flight commander asked me.

"Newbie," (slang for any new guy with less time in country than the person talking to you,) "Have you seen fire yet?"

I shook my head. The pilot smirked, turning the chopper down a river valley. Only ten minutes later, flying at one-hundred feet above the river flow, I saw rifle muzzle flashes. As the bad guys took shots at us.

How special... thank God for not finding any real marksmen with fifty-cal sniper rifles. I thought.

* * *

My unit was HMM 364 (Helicopter Medium Marine)

Known as the Purple Foxes Squadron; consisted of twenty-five pilots, twenty-five copilots, plus the marine crew chiefs, and machine gunners.

The helicopter crews consisted of one flight commander pilot, one co-pilot, one crew chief (the ranking enlisted man in charge of all the mechanical workings of the helicopter,) and two Marines manning the 50 caliber machine guns.

Also on troop deployment, a third Marine operated a 30-caliber machine gun mounted on a tri-pod. His job was to fire out of the cargo/personnel ramp, when needed.

In addition to the combat issued *helmet*, the crew also wore, trousers, boots, a *survival vest*, and a *ceramic shell vest*.

The *survival vest* held items needed to "survive until help arrives, if shot down." Inside the vest was a radio, flares, knife, and personal items.

The *ceramic vest* was a less than perfect bullet deflector, but much thicker than a camo tee shirt.

On mission take-off, it was customary to climb to ten thousand feet, for a short time, just to give the men relief, from the sometimes 160-degree humid temperature, inside the helicopter.

My ride was the Boeing Vertol CH-46 Sea Knight.

It was about 45 feet long and 16 feet high, weighing about 12,000 pounds' empty and 25,000 pounds' max load. Exceeding the latter number, got a lot of flight crews killed.

Twin General Electric turboshaft engines developed 1870 horsepower, each with tandem three-bladed rotors.

There were no windows to look out, or to be shot at, except for the Plexiglas windshield. The Sea Knight was not a racehorse... but was a damn workhorse, when treated with respect.   *   *   *

The frag, assignment officer, would slide our orders, under the door of our Hootch, for the next day's missions.

A routine day for me was to drop off and pick up either troops or supplies, to the field.

Priority daytime flights were for either medevac or recover of troops, from battle zones.

Medevac Emergency flights (life or death) were either day or night, but were the only kind of night flights we would fly.

The medevac helicopter was a great morale boost for the Marines, in the field. They said if they were wounded the chances were good. We would come and get them and transport them to a field medical unit, somewhere close.

A wounded Marine told our crew, while we flew him to the medical unit, that just the sound of our loud whirling engines, brought a smile to his buddies faces.

The fact was that almost all the wounded men, while fighting, were brought out from the combat zone alive, by helicopters. The whirly birds could get them to the hospital usually, under one hour's time.

Several times my crew and I had to fly into "hot" landing zones, to evacuate the wounded troops. This put every person onboard the chopper at risk, becoming casualties ourselves.

It was our job, and with some dumb luck and Devine intervention, we saved many lives.

The medevac flights were even part of the jargon... DUSTOFF, named after Lt. Paul Kelly, killed on a medevac mission, in 1964. The term Dustoff, came from Kelly's radio call sign.

61

MY PERSONAL CLOSE CALLS

Were many... too many!

Looking back, my tour would end up being like a mesh of two Hollywood movies of the day. The first film, with all the terror, blood and guts of 'Platoon.' On almost every night flight, the Viet Cong would shoot at us. The daytime was probably the same also, but we could only see the tracer rounds, coming at us, in the night time. Most of the real action was from the Marble Mountain Marine Base, and the Freedom Hill drop off point for our missions.

The second film, Robin William's dark comedy, with his goofball antics in 'Good Mornin' Vietnam,' was sometimes close to my off duty reality. It is strange how when people are placed into daily life and death situations, they usually need a safety valve to keep from going nuts.

Laughter after all, is the body's natural narcotic to relieve depression and stress.

Next is a list of a few of my CCs (close calls) ... brushes with near death experiences... in no chronological order, or severity in ...

'The Real Vietnam.'

* * *

CC #1: MY FIRST JOHN WAYNE MOMENT: In between missions, we had other duties. One of them was to staff the 'Ready-room,' next to the flight line, where all of the helicopters sat lined up, waiting for their next mission.

We helped assign the crews as needed, looked over some needed paperwork, on my first time in the office.

BOOM! BOOM! Shook the *Ready-room* to its core.

The Viet Cong fired mortar rounds, and blew out several Plexiglas windshields of the helicopters, parked just outside the flimsy sheet metal building.

The radio in the building sounded, a call coming in. I picked up the radio, and answered the call.

It was my commanding officer. He asked me to tell him what I saw.

I told him about the shattered Plexiglas windshields I could see, from inside the building. He ordered me to go outside, and assess how much damage was done to the aircrafts.

Lucky for me, an enlisted crew chief grabbed me by the collar... and pulled me back, inside the 'Ready-room,' as many more mortars were still coming in hot, at the flight line. They would have taken me out for sure.

"Hey dumbshit, get your ass inside." Where were you going?"

"The CO asked me to check and see how much damage there was?"

"He can wait. Plexiglas is cheaper to replace than a greenhorn cowboy!"

An order overruled... a life saved.   MINE!

*   *   *

CC #2: BLOWN ENGINE... PERFECT TIMING SAVED CREW

We were inbound in our C46 loaded heavy, with six-thousand pounds of C-Rats for our troops, in the remote hill country.

I approached the elevated landing zone with all my senses, on full alert. Similar too the year's first NFL regular season games, after a month of pretend practices.

Game Day!

Think of a thousand-foot-high flat top mesa, in the Four Corners area of the U.S. southwest desert. With the same blazing hot temperature, only with ninety-nine percent humidity. The mesa was more like a giant green golf tee.

The mesa's top was barley large enough to land a C46 Marine Helicopter.

Lucky for me, I had taken the time to set up that textbook approach, setting my machine down perfectly square, in the mesa's center.

While pushing the collective down to land, we lost total power, from the number one engine.

I still had enough power from the remaining number two engine, to maintain level flight, but we were too heavy to climb out of any miscalculations, while descending to the landing zone.

Thank God... we settled to the ground like the un-airworthy, ten-ton hunk of meta,l we had just become.

If I had not taken the time to align the chopper absolute perfectly, we would have slid off one side of the mesa, to our deaths.

The recon squads we had come to re-supply, scrambled and unloaded the C-Rats. Now much lighter, the number two engine had enough lift to just get us airborne. I slipped the wounded machine down the side of the mesa, and was able to gain enough airspeed, to achieve level flight.

We limped back and landed safely, at the base flight line. A great time to have done it right, for a change, Ricky boy!

sites.google.com

This was a photo taken two years before I arrived in Country, in May, 1967.

A C46 was shot down by enemy fire. A U.S. Marine sergeant points directions to a group of newly arrived replacement Marines, atop embattled Hill 881, below the demilitarized zone, near the Laotian border, South Vietnam.

* * *

CC #3: FILMING OUR DEATHS... NOT REALLY

I was flying copilot on this mission. We had previously dropped off a recon team in the jungle, when we got a call, that they needed to be extracted ASAP.

My flight commander, Winstrand had backed the helicopter up against the face of a cliff, allowing the six-man recon team to storm aboard the rear loading ramp.

Heavy enemy fire blasted into the chopper.

"Mike! Mike! The recon sergeant yelled to his men.

The Marines returned the enemy fire, with continuous thundering weapons, on full automatic.

My second John Wayne moment was right then.

I neglected my copilot duties, just long enough, to pick up my movie camera and film the battle, from just behind our helicopter's two machine gunners.

Maybe a photographer career in Hollywood later on?

* * *

CC#4 HELICOPTER PILOT DISTRACTION A DEADLY THING

We had been airborne for a couple hours, on a non-descript, but somewhat windy, Vietnam afternoon.

I was in control of the chopper, sitting in the second seat today. Thoughts about the stellar waves forming in the bay, and waiting for me to surf, only minutes from our hooch, at base camp.

It had been a routine mission so far. Except, we were loaded heavy, almost too heavy. Lots of cargo and our maximum number of troops to drop off, at a remote outpost.

For some reason, even after rethinking why it happened, I was in a funk, after putting us on final to the LZ.

We were climbing up the side of a hill, losing lift... When Art took over. "I've got it!" He said.

Art turned us down the hill, milking the collector to gain control.

Just a minute before, we would have crashed into the jungle hillside. We were way too heavy for the big bird's power, to lift safely. The only possible way to right our crash was to gain airspeed.

After gaining control of the falling rock, Art circled around, and came into the LZ with a level approach.

Most of the Marines were none the wiser, about our near disaster. But, our flight chief knew how lucky we all were. He gave me the "are you f... ing kidding me," stare.

Art Blades saved all of our lives, by taking control, after I was distracted.

Rick you're human... I thought, the experience brought me back to earth. And another lesson learned.

*   *   *

CC#5 FROM PASSENGERS TO OUR PROTECTERS
We were inbound, in our H46, to pick up a recon squad, in the remote hill country.

Again, too heavy, I had to approach the elevated landing zone, with all our senses, on full alert. We had to dump fuel, and throw stuff out, just to keep from crashing.

I had just set that up, and was pushing the collective down to land, when we blew out a hydraulic control line.

We did not fall to the ground, like the un-airworthy ten-ton hunk of metal, we had just become. Amazing when hours of training pay off. We settled to earth, with a slight thud. However, we would not go anywhere broken.

The recon squad, we had come to retrieve from their completed mission, was now transformed into our watch dogs, until another airship could reach us.

All the personnel were transported back to base the next day, by two other Sea Nights. Enter the Jolly Green Giant, our heavy armed brut of a lifting helicopter.

It came in with a crew, and removed our wounded bird, back to base camp, for repairs.

Above is a typical Marine encampment in the bush. It was Not the RITZ... but better than no cover at all. The canvas tents would not stop any enemy fire, but keeping the rain somewhat out made life in this human hell more bearable.

62

YEA I FLY THROUGH THE VALLEY OF DEATH

VIETNAM'S VERSION - *A SHAU VALLEY*

Of all the missions, we flew, the *A Shau Valley* was never a fun run. Too many CCs to recall them all, they all blended into one hell on earth. Nobody wanted to recall the nightmares, even today.

The Valley is the gateway to the Ho Chi Minh Trail, defended enthusiastically, by the NVA and VC forces, to the death. Never a white flag, only the red badge of courage. It is close to the Laotian border, made up of several mountains and valleys.

The *A Shau Valley* was the main conduit for supplies, troops, for units of the North Vietnamese Army, and Vietcong, making it a major target for all our military allies. Both sides paid a high price for every inch of terrain acquired, or retained.

The *A Shau Valley* was the scene of fierce fighting, for soldiers on both sides. Having fought in any A Shau Valley missions, gave each Marine a mark of distinction.

Who could forget Operation Apache Snow, also known as Hamburger Hill.

Below are some more jargons, which we used, in the *A Shau Valley* region.

TRIPLE CANOPY was the thick jungle, plants growing at three different levels – on the ground level, intermediate, and high levels.

HOT HOIST meant to lift a Marine, from the ground, by a helicopter using our hoist, due to the triple canopy, while under enemy fire.

We used POP SMOKE to mark a location or target, or a LZ with a smoke grenade of yellow, purple, or green. The bad guys would set off a smoke grenade to lure us in. We coordinated with the ground good-guys which color we should use, to be safe.

RED LZ was for a landing zone, under fire.

The term SANDY, was the navigational name of the northeastern-most corner of the Saigon Flight Information Region. Any mission past that point, meant we got combat pay and combat income tax exemption.

They say it is best to forget the missions made, into *A Shau Valley*. I remembered one, I can't forget. We dropped off a six-man recon squad, and started taking on hellish ground fire, on lift off.

Our flight's seasoned crew chief was critically wounded. Enough said about the *A Shau Valley*.

Looking Dapper!

Later in my hooch... my smart guy gaze... while smoking a pipe... firmly imbedded into COUNTRY, for the duration of my tour. Showing my version of the *'Good Mornin' Vietnam'* attitude.

*   *   *

63

LAND BASED CLOSE CALLS JUST AS FUN... NOT

Crazy times with plenty of things to cry about, sometimes with chemical induced slapstick comedy added into the mix.

* * *

CC#6 PARTY 'TILL WE ALL DROPPED... FOR GOOD.

To help the men have somewhat of a normal life, the base brought in floorshows each month, from all other the Pacific Rim countries, Bob Hope type events from the US, but not as often.

I was hurrying to get ready for a floorshow, with my roommates, when I reached under my bunk to get a pair of Buffalo moccasins, sent to me by my brother-in-law, that I wanted to wear. I saw an alarm clock, with wires coming out the back right, where my moccasins rested.

Looking up under my bed for my rawhide slippers, I saw prima-cord weaved through the box springs, on my bunk. Prima-cord was a fuse like material for bombs.

The timer was set to go off after we would have returned, to our Quonset hut, from the floor show.

I called the E.O.D. (explosive ordnance disposal) guys and they removed the bomb from our hut.

Because of Washington's need to be politically correct, the military, in Vietnam, was charged to hire local labor to do some maintenance and clean up around the base. They had the freedom to roam the base and wreak havoc, unchecked.

The bad guys in Nam did not wear color coordinated uniforms, like the enemy did in World War Two. So it was a crapshoot, every day locals wandered around the base blending in, looking to do what???

* * *

Above I'm doing a preflight to the outside of the helicopter.

CC#7: PREFLIGHT OR SOON DIE

Another day I was inside my helicopter, going over my preflight at the flight line. I saw a large Planters Peanut can. I started to toss it out of the chopper, but the weight made me stop.

Inside I found a hand-frag (a fragmentation grenade to be thrown by a soldier,) with its safety pin pulled out.

The grenade's squeeze lever was held in place, by the walls of the tin can.

As long as the lever was squeezed tight, against the grenade's side, the fuse would not start to explode the fragmentation bomb.

It was safe to handle, but once the lever is released, there are only about three to five seconds to duck out of the way, before all hell breaks loose.

If we had taken off, and the can rolled over, the grenade would have slipped out, and blown the whole crew and helicopter to bloody bits.

I called the E.O.D. and they disposed of the peanut can and its kiss of death.

*   *   *

CC#8: TOUCHED BY AN ANGEL

Sometimes no matter how hard I tried to screw up...

I could fall into the honey-dipper's cleaning bucket, and come out smelling like a water lily, on the Mekong River.

We had a big floorshow and rap-up party the night before. A non-drinking pilot, from Utah, and me were the only pilots the Frag officer could wake up, in time to fly a rescue mission.

The non-drinking pilot was a greenhorn, and unfamiliar with the area we needed to travel, to bring the others home.

I showed him how to do the pre-flight, at freedom Hill, and to get the coordinates for the recon team rescue.

I passed out on takeoff. The greenhorn pilot earned his wings that night. Guarding angel wings for me, and the rescued Marines. When I awoke the trip was over.

I figured later, though I was unable to partake consciously, in the mission, I was still the one to give the greenhorn good info.

A flight mission earned, while I slept like a snoring baby Snuffy. Right-place right-time.

* * *

64

OTHER CRAZY STUFF I DID OR SAW IN NAM

I was about to play flag football, after having done 1000 sit-ups, just before the start of the game. Bending down, to get into a football stance, my back locked up. I could not straighten up. I was less than two months from completing my tour in Nam, and I wasn't allowed to fly for a month.

The thirty days of boredom, from being grounded, allowed me to witness some real lame things.

Lame thing #1: A drunken Major Gary Piddock jumped up, and emptied his 38 into the ceiling of our Hootch. The next day was a torrential downpour, with water pouring through the bullet holes, in the canvas roofing material.

Lame thing #2: Another drunken pilot McCry (Pig was his duly earned nickname for manners and appearance) ran up on the stage, at the floor show, and made a fool of himself.

Not a high mark for all of the other pilots, watching one of their own, slobber all over the performers, in the floor show.

Lame thing #3: We had some floorshows called Round-Eye-Show, no Asians allowed on stage. Not PC but we had our fill of slanted eyes always staring at us, either plotting to kill us, or just envious of our life styles. Both of them made us uneasy, when being watched.

Lame thing #4: Somehow 262 Christmas trees where spread out around our tropical encampment. Shows how boring off-time could become, when I took the time to count them all.

Lame thing #5: After coming back from another late night at a floorshow, I awoke the next morning, planning to head towards the mailroom. Just about that same time, shrapnel from an explosion flew into, and all around the mailroom, wounding forty-six Navy sailors and Marines.

Maybe one of the performers, not allowed onto the floorshow, Round-eyed evening, had their pound of revenge.

One time I was glad that I hadn't been the early bird, looking for the worm (my mail from home)

*　*　*

65

FREE AT LAST... FREE AT LAST... FOR A TIME

After months of insanity, I had earned my first R & R.

And of course, all us jar heads looked forward to the rest-and-recreation vacations. They were given to all hands, and had to be taken during our one-year duty tour, in Vietnam.

Out-of-country R & R's could be used in Bangkok, Hawaii, Tokyo, Australia, Hong Kong, Manila, Penang, Taipei, Kuala Lampur, or Singapore.

My first seven-day R&R was to Hawaii. I was relaxing in the passenger seat of the jeep, driven by the Marine assigned to get me to the airport. As a bonus, the day was pleasant, with almost bearable heat and humidity.

I should have thought it was too good to be true. Kay would be waiting to spoil me with all the Hawaiian goodies, with lots of one-on-one married couple gyrations for sure. And not to mention the four to five-foot ocean waves, waiting for me to conquer.

The jeep lurched to the right. I came back to the present, long enough to see a Vietcong, wearing civilian clothes, of course, pointing and firing his AK 47 at us.

The marine stomped down on the gas pedal, his foot almost going through the floorboard.

The under-powered military vehicle came to life, roaring forward, following the driver's lead.

It was over. Not on a scale with my flight missions. But come on... give me a break for crying out loud!

With a quick glance over my shoulder, I saw that the snake of a man had crawled back, into the jungle.

"Not fair Sir! Your R and R and all!" yelled the Marine over the revved engine, as we bounded along.

"Like love and war is? Get me to the airfield Snuffy," I said, winking at him.

I looked at the driver again, as he stared ahead, looking for any more trouble.

I thought he and I were more alike than different. Here we were a commissioned officer and enlisted grunt, riding side by side, in a rolling death trap. The VC bullet could have killed either one of us, regardless of our rank.

But after all, we were SEMPRE FI (The shortened Latin phrase for 'Always Faithful.') Snuffys, the marine motto, covering all ranks.

Always to 'look out for each other.'

We hit a hard bump, jarring me back to the moment. So much for a break from this insanity, and my pleasant thoughts of Kay's planned surprises.

My only respite would be, after the transport plane flew out of this country's air space. Several planes had been the victims of a ground to air missile strike. On second thought, respite would be when I was out of the range, of any North Vietnam, or smuggled Chinese missiles.

* * *

BUT THEN IT WAS OVER

My **IN-COUNTRY** was over... a one-year tour consisting of 600 flight missions. My best friend, met me at the Honolulu Airport, with open arms. We started our life of togetherness, free from someone else calling the shots, for our future.

Kay meeting me at the airport in Hawaii, my hell in Nam was a fading memory, for the most part.

Television brought the brutality of war, into the comfort of the living room. Vietnam was lost in the living rooms of America–not on the battlefields of Vietnam.

–Marshall McLuhan, 1975

*   *   *

PART 7

SEVENTH HEAVEN

66
BACK TO THE PRESENT DAY

December, 21 1970

The constant ocean swell caused the long surfboard to rise and fall, like a smooth ride on a fast running stallion.

I pressed my inner thighs tight against the surfboard, to remain upright.

A loud roar of an approaching jet airplane, from the Marine Base, made me turn and watch the fighter lift up and head out to sea. The jet's fiery afterburning caught my attention. I came back to the now.

I laughed again, "I give up... too funny."

* * *

I returned to where Kay was laying on the blanket.

After dropping my surfboard on the warm sand, I sat down next to her. "Catch any good rides?" Kay asked.

The two young people on horseback caught my eye again. They had dismounted and were walking their mounts down the paved highway away from us.

"Earth to Rick!"

"Oh sorry babe... yeah a few good sets," I said rolling over on my back.

"Turn over I'll oil up your back... lobster man."

I did as instructed, and said, "Lots of memories out there."

"Any about me cowboy?"

"All the good ones. The others a mixed bag."

Me catching some waves on Waimea Beach

My favorite surfboard I used in Hawaii

Above is a pic of our good-bye party from Hawaii, sending us off on a new life style and to the good ole U.S.A. mainland.

After spending the last eighteen months in paradise, we left Waimea Bay Hawaii and flew to El Toro Marine Base in California, where I mustered out of the Marine Corps. I was a civilian again, but with no job. Kay and I drove an old Chrysler from El Toro, Marine Base in Southern California back to Wenatchee, Washington.

In the months of November and December, I got to ski every day. My need to catch up on snow skiing was my new boss. In my list of what mattered now, skiing the number one event away from my family. How sweet the cold mountain air was on my sunbaked skin. I loved being in the tropics, but nothing matched fresh crisp air filling my lungs.

Still unemployed, we drove to Whidbey Island once a month to visit family and friends.

66

BACK IN THE GOOD OLE U.S.A. MAINLAND.

Now that we were back in the continental United States State, I had a couple of loose ends that needed my attention.

The first was if Rego was still alive and well.

The banker's wife had sold Rego and I was trying to track him down.

I wrote the guy in Twisp, where Rego was pastured. The man thought the letter from Rick Grimstead was from a kid. In his response, not wanting to make me cry, he wrote me saying he didn't know about Rego.

I called him and said, "I'm a Washington State Trooper and an old guy now."

The man sighed and said, "Oh oh... we had a really tough winter and the old horse died."

I thanked him and put the phone down.

Rest in peace ole boy... hope there is some grass lands in heaven, I thought. The news of losing my best friend, non-human, in my formative years, made me realize how life takes no prisoners. Like is for the living, and I had better get on my being the best hubby and best daddy I could.

* * *

I Applied to the FBI and was told that no white guys, regardless of qualification, would be needed for a least a year. And probably would be a longer time than that.

Next I talked to a guy working for the ATF. He told me if I got in, I would be stationed in either Chicago or Detroit.

That was not in my wheelhouse for places to live.

So, without any real options, I followed my dad's lead and joined the Washington State Patrol in Kelso, WA.

* * *

67

WASHINGTON STATE PATROL

I spent the next twenty years as a Washington State Patrolman. Below is my official Washington State Trooper gradation photo 1974.

At the top boys and me in 1974
Below are my Mom, Kay and the boys.

I had many different looking rides in the Patrol, over the years serving in the Burlington and Whidbey Island offices as a patrolman and as a sergeant in Tacoma.

Kay, me, my Uncle Chester, sisters Gail and Chris.

* * *

Like while serving in the Marine Corps, I had several memorable events in the Washington State Patrol. Some of the events were a direct danger to me, others involved helping people in need of life saving assistance.

While working late at night, as a patrolman on the Washington State Patrol on Whidbey Island, I stopped to help a woman in a broken down car. I was standing next to the driver's window talking to the woman when a car raced towards us out of the dark. Too late to duck out of the way, I turned sideways just in time. The car roared past, at about sixty miles per hour, striking the bellowed out crease in my trooper pants.

A couple inches closer, the car would have struck and shattered my legs before killing me. The car missed the curve fifty feet ahead and crashed into the trees off of the highway.

The car's airbags deployed and the panicking driver was unhurt except for her mental state. She told me she was lost, and while looking to see out of the side windows her shoe got stuck into the floor mat forcing the gas pedal down.

* * *

Another time, again late at night, I came upon a one car accident. The driver had plowed into some heavy brush and looked to be unconscious, but she had no signs of any bodily damage. I did a quick exam of her condition and discovered she was not breathing.

After sliding her out of the car onto the ground, I gave her mouth to mouth recitation, until she took in a deep breath and could breathe on her own.

When the paramedics showed up and we got her to the hospital and stabilized. I had her do a breath analyzer test. She scored .50 on the breath analyzer.

The nurse at the hospital told me that a person with a score of .30 to .40 is extremely at life threatening condition. They would most likely have complete unconsciousness or might pass out suddenly and can't be awakened. Coma is possible. This is the level of surgical anesthesia. Death may occur.

And the real kicker, the score over 0.45 BAC death will occur in most people. Looks like the lady was lucky someone found her in time.

* * *

Another time, while the patrolling late at night, near La Conner, on Pull-and-Be-Damned Road leading towards the Swinomish Indian Reservation. I drove up on two women passed out in a car that had slid into a ditch.

Pull-and-Be-Damned was the actual name of the road. An old description about its name says it best. *'The road was so steep that when raining a person needed to hitch some horses, to pull a cart behind you, and to keep from being stuck in the mud. But since you were pulling stuff in the rain you were damned already.'*

The same drill as with the first intoxicated woman only times two. And again... another hour of the alcohol working on them, without any help, and they too may have not made it back.

* * *

Yet again, I came across a Tacoma Native American couple and their son was choking on something he had eatin.

I gave the boy the Heimlich maneuver and back blows. He spat out the food and started breathing again. And I did the same maneuver again later with Nancy Crook, a close friend of ours.

*   *   *

State Patrol will honor troopers

The News Tribune

State trooper John Martin of Olympia, a 10-year veteran of the State Patrol, will be honored Wednesday as trooper of the year during ceremonies at the Washington State Patrol Academy.

Other awards will go to trooper Billy Jeffries of Seattle and citizen Robert Kimsey for stopping a suicide attempt on the Pacific Highway South bridge over State Route 518 near Seattle.

Also receiving an award will be Sgt. Richard Grimstead of Tacoma, who cleared the air passage and restored breathing to a child choking on a piece of candy.

Also during the ceremony, a commendation will be presented to Sgt. Brian Holliday, Trooper Karey Reisdorph and communications officer Susan Jackson, all of Tacoma, for coming to the aid of a fellow trooper who suffered a near-fatal reaction to medication.

SERGEANT RICHARD F. GRIMSTEAD

CHIEF'S AWARD FOR PROFESSIONAL EXCELLENCE

Sergeant Richard F. Grimstead gave the ultimate gift when he performed life-saving emergency assistance to a child who was choking on a piece of candy. Today, we honor Sergeant Grimstead for his professional response in an emergency situation.

In the afternoon of December 28, 1990, Sergeant Grimstead was approached by a distraught father who sought his assistance in providing emergency treatment to his son. Sergeant Grimstead found the mother and child at the side of the market, where he was contacted by the father. The mother was endeavoring to dislodge a piece of candy from the child's throat with a series of back slaps, which proved to be ineffective. Sergeant Grimstead quickly assessed that the child was not breathing, his face was cyanotic in color, and there was bleeding from the mouth and nose. He took the frightened child from his mother and administered a series of four to five abdominal thrusts, to no effect. After attempting to retrieve the candy with his finger without result, he reversed the direction and was able to push the obstruction down the child's throat, clearing the airway and restoring normal respiration.

Aid was summoned to the scene; the child was taken to the family doctor, who found that the child had suffered no trauma to his throat and no apparent injury had occurred. The medical personnel indicated it is almost certain that without Sergeant Grimstead's efforts and professionalism in administering emergency first aid, this child would have expired at the scene.

By his precise action in preventing a tragic loss to this family, Sergeant Grimstead demonstrated his commitment to public service and performed to the highest expectations of the department.

I don't claim to be called a hero. All of the things I did was because of my training and I just wanted to do a good job protecting and serving others in need.

* * *

I'm standing in the center front of my detachment photo, while serving as the sergeant for the State Patrol.

* * *

It's strange how a nasty car accident, can end up being a blessing of sorts. I could ride off into the sunset, on a brand-new Harley motorcycle!

All because of my Whidbey Island head-on mishap. I was south bound on Highway 20, heading for Oak Harbor, when a man in a one-ton cargo van, hit me head-on, going 55 mph. I had fractured some ribs, and was on the police radio talking to the dispatcher, in almost a whisper, saying I had an accident, and to please send some backup.

I must have sounded critical, because I was soon surrounded by all the on-duty patrol units. I was pinned inside my patrol car, between the deployed airbag, steering wheel, and center plywood console. I had broken several ribs, and breathing was difficult.

The driver of the van that hit me, was not the cause of the accident. A semi-truck had missed his turnoff, and had backed up his trailer onto a cross street, but his cab stuck out, into the traffic lane. The van driver had almost hit the semi-truck's cab, whipping to go around, when he hit me head-on. The van driver was unhurt.

The good news, after I recouped from broken ribs, the semi-truck company paid my hospital bills and paid me a cash settlement, which I used to buy my first Harley.

Adam traded a rib for a wife, I traded a couple of broken ribs, in exchange for my new iron horse.

* * *

STATE PATROL 1984

The State Patrol wanted to see if adding helicopters to the aerial traffic division was something to consider. For six months, I was assigned to fly the Bell chopper.

On some days, I would fly in, and investigate an accident, then take off and go to the next incident.

Here I am filming a Washington State Patrol promotion on the use of helicopters, in the Special Divisions Unit.

I was told that because of a funding issue, after less than one year of testing. the helicopter part of the aerial enforcement unit was scraped.

*   *   *

68

SHERIFF TIME

I retired from the State Patrol in 2001, and was elected twice as the Skagit County Sheriff, in 2003 and 2007.

On my first day in office, I stood at the front of the Sheriff's headquarters meeting room, and spelled out my vision and directions to the other officers and office staff.

I chose to proudly wear the standard Sheriff's uniform, instead of the big shot suit and tie, worn by many upper level police administrators. I was sending my deputies a message of support, showing them that I was not just a boss in a suit, but a fellow solider in arms, against the bad guys.

Below is a reprint from an interview I did for CJDS

(Criminal Justice Degree Schools) *"I was commissioned as a State Trooper in December 1974, and then was promoted to Sergeant in 1989. As Sergeant you oversee a detachment of 6-12 State Troopers. Overall, I spent 28 years in the State Patrol and retired in 2001 with most of time in Oak Harbor, following a stint in Tacoma. When I retired, several people suggested that I run for Skagit County Sheriff. I was elected in 2002 and started as Sheriff in 2003 for two terms."*

Four years later, I stood with my family for a photo, on winning second term election campaign.

Dave Brunson, Wayne Dowhaniuk and Gary Shand.

I was so blessed to have so many friends and supporters. It would have been impossible without their due diligence, and advice, along the way.

Thanks guys and gals!!!

Above is one of the many yard signs, disbursed by my loyal supporters.

I was kinda swept up, in a grass roots movement, to have my name put on the ballot for the Skagit County Sheriff's office in 2003. The seating Sheriff had decided to retire, and had already given his support for one of his officers to take his place.

Thanks to the community support, and the work of my tireless volunteers and friends, I was elected as an outsider, by one of the largest margins of victory, in recent times.

Re-election was another matter, and not as much fun as the first. I had become the dreaded incumbent to a few, as in all political campaigns. Over all, it ended up being a good experience. I have some enduring memories, especially with my staff and officers.

It was my pleasure, and a good ride, on my metal horse named Harley, leading the Moving Wall Vietnam parade down Interstate 5, to the Burlington Softball fields, for a gathering of local veterans.

* * *

When I have been asked to reflect on my time in the Sheriff's office, and share what I found to be the most compelling, one event trumps them all.

Nine days before the seventh anniversary of the most horrific terrorist attack in U.S. history, September 11, 2001, a lone madman ended the lives of six innocent Americans, including the life of a brave law enforcement officer.

Skagit County Sheriff's Deputy, Anne Jackson, was one of the six victims in a Sept. 2nd shooting rampage, that began in the small northwest Washington community of Alger, and continued in a high-speed chase down Interstate 5.

On September 9, 2008, in the twilight days of my long public career, I led the service of 4,000 mourners, who attended Deputy Jackson's memorial.

Anne and I shared a love of horses, and we often talked about animals. I remembered her dry sense of humor and called her a "precious warrior."

Her death, was called the end of her watch, on the Officer Down Memorial Page. Over four thousand mourners, packed into the Burlington Edison High School Stadium, under a cloudless summer sky, to remember Jackson.

I performed the hardest task I have even done, while a law officer, by handing Anne Jackson's mother, the flag of honor, bestowed upon her murdered daughter.

*   *   *

69

MARINE RESERVES

Change of command in Whidbey... 1983

I served in the Marine Reserves for 36 years... 1965 through 2003. After the Reserves moved the helicopters out of the Whidbey Base in 1981, our unit became the headquarters for the Maintenance Operation for the A6 jets on base. In 1983 I became the commander of that unit.

* * *

On the next page I'm sitting inside my Reserve Unit helicopter wearing my, not so standard, Marine Reserves flight helmet. Notice the SKI USA on the front. Just in case, I needed to put down and rescue a fallen comrade, on the Mt. Baker Ski slopes.

My helmet, I'm wearing was used in the Hollywood movie *Officer and a Gentleman,* which was filmed on the Whidbey Base, as well as in Port Townsend. I lent my helmet to the actor that wore it, when he plunged into the *Dilbert Dunker* at the Naval Training facility for the film

A different Dilbert Dunker but similar to the one depicted in the movie.

* * *

The Burlington School District asked the Marine Reserves to send a helicopter to Allen Elementary School. The purpose was to let the children see a military helicopter close up, and have the pilot available to answer their questions.

With Kay being a teacher at Allen school, it made good sense for me to make the trip. I was glad to fly my bird in, for good of the country. Notice how slim the pilot was!

The vast grass playground, void of any children's activities, made a perfect landing zone to display the helicopter for the kid's inspection.

After going inside the school, I spent a while sharing questions and answers with inquisitive students' in Kay's classroom.

On my last flight for the Marine Reserves, in 1981, I had forgotten my lunch box, or something, and landed my helicopter in our Bayview home back yard, to say hello.

*   *   *

68
NO SLOW-MO SKIING

My skiing adventures as an adult... sort of an oxymoron Rick Grimstead and the word SLOW. Here I am, in Big Mountain, Montana, ready to take off down black diamond runs, or blast through snow packed tree lines.

Kay was always ready for a little skiing.

I was more of a "Just-One-More-Fun-Run sort of Guy!

Here Kay and I are with Darren and Eric, in 1979, off on
one of our many skiing adventures.

Sometimes it was a quick trip to Mount Baker, Stevens
Pass or an overnight train trip to Big Mountain, Montana,
complete with some delays, because of avalanches across the
tracks. My versions of forced family fun usually turned out
to be a good time had by all. At least that's how I
remembered them.

My short-term memory is sometimes lacking, but the
farther back I think, the clearer the details seem. Just sayin'.

I had just a few good runs during the Police Winter
Olympics in Heavenly Valley, California. Winning two Gold,
two Silver and a Bonze metal or two. Not bad for an old guy
with the heart of a teenager for fun.

*   *   *

69

HUNTING-HORSEBACK RIDING-FISHING-BIKING

I did some shooting... hunting, fishing and big boy bike riding while enjoying time off from my police duties.

Sightin' in ole Blunder Bust!

Wyoming horseback Elk hunt

A 1985 *Alaskan Bush People* type hunt and escape.

My favorite bird, *The Pheasant*, one prized rooster that didn't get away. The great white hunter blasting the beast... to the ground, just out of our back door, near the driveway.

A bird in the hand, or a fish in the boat, is worth less than the money spent to get them. But life is about the thrill of the hunt, more than stupid required pieces of green colored paper. Nice to not worry about the paper thing in retirement.

Below are a couple of real hogs I latched onto!

A Forty pound plus King Salmon, a slightly heavier angler. Butchering a pig after an easy, faux, hunt behind the barn.

*   *   *

RIDING WITH MY LOVES

My Biker Babe and Me

Fat Boys and Harleys Rule

There are a few possible pit falls when riding behind me, on my Harley. This year, while on a safety first, towing the bike behind us in a trailer, until needed adventure, we reached a scenic, low risk of heavy traffic, cruising area. I proudly unloaded the iron horse from its trailer, and off we went.

This year on the very first day of our easy ride, in the Rocky Mountain National Park, I glided to a stop for a restroom break. The word *break* came home to roast, when we were saddling back up, onto the bike. Kay lost her balance, just for an instant, falling off the Harley, breaking her shoulder.

Her reward, for riding tandem behind her Prince, not-so, charming motorcycle guy, was a first class ambulance, sirens blazing, trip to the Estes Park Hospital.

*   *   *

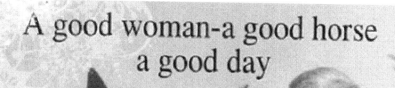

A good woman-a good horse a good day

70

THE REAL RICK

To any naysayers who might read this story, I love my family and my friends. I have never placed anyone at risk while doing fun things, at least the things I try, which look like fun to me. However, it may be a little off base and dangerous to others?

Life is Good!

Kay and I are WSU Cougar fans through and through.

Wikipedia says: Founded in 1890, WSU (colloquially "Wazzu") is the state's **land-grant** university, well known for its programs in chemical engineering, veterinary medicine, agriculture, pharmacy, neuroscience, food science, plant science, business, architecture, and communications.

It is ranked in the top 140 universities in America, with high research activity, with almost 30,000 student enrollment today, including the grad programs. Second only to the University of Washington in student enrollment...

But in NOTHING ELSE!

The charm of the remote campus, located in the *Palouse region* by Pullman, Washington makes every Cougar football game, a long *road-game* for the alumni of Western Washington.

Over the years, we went to many WSU games, home and away. Below we are with our traveling buds, Nancy Krook and Mike Youngquist. Their mates Jeanne Youngquist took the photo of us, while Frank Krook was probably rounding up some adult beverages for our clan.

Which reminded me of our flight, we took to Phoenix, to take on the Arizona State Sun Devils.

After deplaning from our flight from Seattle, the guys hung out at the Sky Harbor International airport in Phoenix, waiting for the gals to return from using the restrooms.

Jeanne had brought this real cool large Cougar flag, with a telescoping feature. At the football games, she would stand with the flag rolled around the metal pole, and whip it as if casting a large surf fishing pole. The pole would extend unrolling the flag all in one smooth move. The Cougar fans would yell their approval, at the waving WSU battle flag.

Well... in another not as so cool move, I picked up the flag pole, without the flag attached, and began to show off my pole-snapping skills, in the middle of the airport. I pulled the flagpole over my head and snapped it forward, telescoping the pole to a sword thrusting position. Think of a swashbuckling pirate, stabbing a foe, in front of him.

The first couple of times I pulled it off, to Frank and Mike's laughter of approval.

My third attempt at fame was not **a charm**.

The pole's pointed metal ferrule end came loose, becoming a projectile, flying through the crowded deplaning area, and impelling itself deep into a small leather suitcase, on the floor, between two seated Catholic nuns.

"Oh my lord," the nun exclaimed.

At first lost for words... I gathered my thoughts, and ran to the nun's aid. "I'm so sorry sister... it got away from...

The nun cut me off and laughed. "It's ok son, boys will be boys. Want your dart back?"

Kay, Nancy and Jeanne walked back, just in time, to see the result of my athletic prowess, once again.

We shared a good laugh at my well-deserved expense.

* * *

71

My Family

Family is always first with our Grimstead clan:
By the tree: Darren and Dina   Eric and Kristal.
Madison in the center,
Grandma Kay, Gabby, Drew, Grandpa Rick, Hunter and Chase.

Granddaughter Gabby pulls at my vest and heartstrings.

Eric and Darren stand side by side with proud Pa!

HANGING WITH MY BEST FRIEND

Alaskan Ferry Fun Times

Hiking Cascade Ridge

Arizona Golfing the snow birds have arrived!

On our way to the nineteenth hole for a little bubbly
or at least something a little stronger than green tea

Unlike the goals for the game of Golf... all of Rick's stories were well over par for the course, and that was a good thing!

NOT THE END - HAPPY TRAILS AHEAD TO EVERYONE!

72

AUTHOR'S NOTE

CAN RICKY COME OUT AND PLAY?

I would like to say what a privilege it was to compile Rick's story. Thank you Kay and Rick Grimstead for all of your insights, ideas, needed corrections, understanding of my vision for how to reveal his great adventures, and most of all your total patience.

It was for a real labor-of-love, on my part.

Whenever I would get together with some of Rick's close friends, his unbelievable stories would eventually come up.

They would say someone needs to write these stories down... it would make a great book. However, the wild things Rick accomplished in his life, seemed more like material for a fiction novel, than a sure enough good-ole-boy, real life story.

Aww shucks... it makes me want to tear up, but all kidding aside... for real.

Do you ever wonder why some old men become cranky, yelling at the kid, just crossing their yard? And why some macho types, go around trying to impress others, with their tough guy attitude?

Some would say they need to get in touch with their feminine side. Also, the only difference between men and little boys, is the price of their toys. Closer-to-the-truth. I believe Richard Forbes Grimstead discovered not the... *fountain of youth,* but the *secret of staying young.*

In a person's mind for sure... remember the saying... *mind-over-m*atter? No *matter* if your body is a little flabby.

It goes something like this... let the little boy inside of you, see and enjoy the wonders of the world. And never look through the *old man's microscope* at events, or people right in front of you. In short, be a kid, enjoy Christmas morning every day.

Always be a grownup with all decisions involving others, but when it's just you... let Ricky come outside to play?

This book and story may be the end of this chapter of Rick's life, but I sense a baker's dozen or so, of more unbelievable adventures, still to unfold, for all of his spellbound family and friends to witness, or hear about.

Love ya

Michael (Mikey) Cannon

40139673R10150

Made in the USA
San Bernardino, CA
12 October 2016